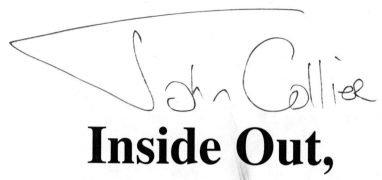

Inside Out,

A Father's Love

By

John Richard Collier

PRESS

Inside Out,
A Father's Love
by John Richard Collier

Printed in the United States of America

ISBN 978-1-60477-340-8

www.xulonpress.com

Dedication

This book is dedicated to the memory of Robert A. Hall. He was my mentor, teacher, and dear friend who led me to Christ and was always leading me by his example. I also dedicate this book to the memory of Richard Amo. He was a bright light in a dark place when I first met him. He became a spiritual father and he was my dear friend in Christ. He is dearly missed as well.

Special Thanks

I would like to thank Andrea DeCento of Twin Rivers Worship Center in Fenton, Missouri for her encouragement and confirmation that this story needs to be told. Her advice and wisdom comes as an editor for several books and publications through the ministry she serves each day.

I also want to thank Charlene Heim of Traverse City, Michigan for her editing contributions in the final days and hours before the final manuscript was submitted. God was gracious to bring these people into my life to fulfill a vision he gave me.

Chapter 1

It was the summer of 1980 and I had graduated from college the previous year with a bachelor's degree in Criminal Justice. I was pursuing a dream of a career in law enforcement with the state police. I had been working in a juvenile detention home for almost three years while going to college, and now that I had graduated I was excited about pursuing my career in law enforcement. The first step would be to attend the State Police academy. I had taken the written exams for the Michigan and Indiana State Police, gone through the background checks, and interviewed with each department.

Now at the age of 23 I had overcome the world on my own. At least that is how I saw it then. I had been an overachiever, setting goal after goal from my teen years to adulthood, excelling in every-thing I did. I loved physical fitness, and was very athletic. I received honors and awards in football and basketball. I was an honor student in high school, was a member of the National Honor Society, a Junior Rotarian, and I had a gift for music and theatre. I had an attitude that I could conquer whatever I wanted to. I was very outgoing, but not the type of person who sought the approval of my peers. On the contrary, I sought the approval of adults, especially those I thought of as father figures and mentors. I had a small circle of close friends, but I was not a trusting person, and letting a person get close to me was something I rarely allowed to happen. I was promiscuous, selfish, and self-serving on the inside. The only things that mattered to me were the personal goals I had set for myself, and since about the age of 12 I knew I would become a police officer.

During my high school and college years I loved playing football and was very active in music and theatre. Music was also a passion for me. I loved to sing and studied voice during high school and then when attending college. It filled a void inside me and it was a world filled with beauty and grace. In high school it brought out another side to me. It was a world I liked to be in, one of singing and acting in school musicals. It was a world of make-believe that allowed me to release deep feelings and emotions that I rarely shared or showed to anyone. Singing with a group of other students known as the GVSU Singers gave me a family of other students during my college years. I was fortunate to study voice under Leslie Eitzen, who was a mezzo soprano of the New York Metropolitan Opera before she became a teacher. And William Beidler was my instructor and leader of the GVSU Singers. Every day I spent in rehearsals getting to know him and my fellow students. We were like children to him, and in many ways he was like a father to us. He was a gifted man who had performed for years on Broadway singing and dancing. In the early days of television he was a young student at the University of Chicago, and on weekends he made money singing live television for NBC television. After college he became very successful in New York, marrying a model and traveling with Broadway companies by train around the country. In the show business world of New York he had associations with famous people such as Jose Farrar and Rosemary Clooney. Later in his career he turned to teaching, and when Bill Beidler became my teacher he also became a father figure and my friend. For years I would affectionately call him my adopted father. Throughout college he taught us how to sing and dance, perform with grace, and he brought out the best in me.

During my second year of college I began to work part-time at the Kent County Juvenile Detention Center as a Child Care Worker. I had a few college buddies who worked there and it was a good part-time job. We were basically jailers for juveniles. Many were hard cases, but there were also kids who were scared runaways. It was a mix of good and bad. The most common thing between all of the juveniles was that they came from poor homes. They suffered from abuse and neglect, and many like me grew up without a father. I could relate to them on many different levels. I knew what it was like to grow up without a father, without much to live on, and in poor neighborhoods. But I was not there to save them. I had my plans for my life mapped out and I was determined to become a state trooper. It had been my plan and I was not going to change it.

Although I had wanted to stay in Michigan and attend the academy in East Lansing there had been a hiring freeze. The opportunity came to go to Indiana in August when I received a letter inviting me to attend the 40th Recruit Class of the Indiana State Police. I was pumped, and my friends and co-workers were excited for me. My dream was about to become a reality, and I couldn't wait to make the trip to Indiana to begin this new chapter in my life. My friends and co-workers celebrated my departure with me before leaving Michigan. I was congratulated by judges and probation officers in addition to my co-workers.

I would be expected to be at the academy Sundays by 5:00 pm, and dismissed on Fridays at 4:00 pm to go home on weekends. I remember showing up early that first Sunday in September 1980 at the Quartermaster to pick up my uniforms, and then proceed to the academy to sign in and take my room assignment with two other cadets. That evening we were called into the gymnasium to line up for roll call. We were told exactly how we would line up each day in military formation for inspection and physical training (PT). We were also told what would be expected of us in the weeks to come, including the news that approximately 15 to 20 percent of the class would drop out before the end of the 16 weeks. The team of officers that would train us would show no mercy, and everyone, including the women, would have to pull their own weight. Training would be rigorous and tough. They only wanted the best, those that were willing to give everything physically and mentally for this great challenge.

That first night I barely got any sleep. My roommates were up until 3:00 am shining their shoes and brass buttons for the uniforms. By 5:00 am everyone was out of bed and lined up in the mess hall for breakfast. Everyone kept their mouths shut as we filed through the breakfast lines for food. We had a short time to eat before falling in for uniform inspection, and then attend training classes through the morning, followed by a quick lunch, and marching outdoors until afternoon classes. We did everything as a single group, and the training officers would jump down the throats of any stragglers. Training during the day wasn't too bad, until we finished our last class and were told we had ten minutes to change into PT gear and be lined up in formation. We would dash off to our rooms to change and find them completely trashed by troopers that conducted inspections. It didn't matter that first week if every crease was perfect and things were shiny and clean. They worked us over mentally as well as physically. That's when the fun began.

The trooper in charge of physical training was Sergeant White. He was like a well-oiled machine, barking out orders, running the cadets through push-ups and calisthenics, running and pushing us until we dropped. He did everything with us, screaming at us that if he could do it we could. I came to the academy prepared physically, so I was able to hang tough and carry my own. I had worked out through the summer months on a daily basis and I enjoyed physical challenges. It was evident for those who were not prepared as they dropped like flies, some falling out in exhaustion. At the conclusion of PT, which was about 90 minutes, we would line up in formation, begin to march, and pick it up to a run. Cadets would fall out to vomit, then get back in formation to continue. Sergeant White would bark out cadence, and training officers on each side would be screaming at cadets to pick it up.

I found out that they were right about the drop-out rate. By Wednesday both of my roommates had quit the academy, and by Thursday of the first week I had two new roommates. Both were former military men. I would learn a lot from them in the coming weeks. They would turn out to be two of the best recruits in the academy.

Everything was regimented and extremely strict. Training consisted of how to dress, walk, talk, march, drive cars in pursuit, use firearms, subdue suspects, and we were instructed on how to maintain a strict *Code of Conduct*. In the classroom we were taught on all aspects of criminal and traffic laws, and we were tested weekly. We were reminded on many occasions that we represented the State of Indiana, and that as state troopers we were to habitually treat everyone with courtesy and respect. Our overall ranking in the class was determined by our academic standing and physical training. We could never take it for granted that we had it made. Week after week the training was grueling, but we became strong as a unit, more confident in ourselves, and growing hungry for the day that we would graduate and receive our appointments.

By the 12th week we received our first night of *"liberty,"* which was a night in the middle of the week where we actually had the chance to go off of the academy grounds and have some fun. A majority, including myself, went out to drink and revel, celebrating one night of freedom. By the end of the week we learned that taking too much liberty wasn't good, as at least two of the cadets were dismissed from the academy for their personal conduct.

I grew to admire Sgt. White, especially through those last few weeks of the academy. He was tough, but fair, and he constantly reminded us of our responsibilities and what we represented. He told us that as police officers we lived in glass houses. In our public and private lives everyone watched us, and would always see us for what we represented. One day I would realize exactly what he meant.

(Indiana State Police Photo of John during Academy training)

By week 15 the state police board and the superintendent came to the academy to conduct interviews before we graduated. We were called into a room one at a time to face them, standing at attention, answering questions regarding our performance during recruit school, about any problems, our past, and our future. When I faced the board and the superintendent my father was in prison at the time. He had been in prison about a year (his second time in the Michigan prison system) for forging prescription drugs. The last time I had seen him was during his court proceedings before he was sent back into the system. He had become controlled by drugs and had a serious addiction problem. During the background investigation that the state police conducted on me before I was invited to recruit school they learned of my father and his past. I remember being questioned about my father and his criminal background. I was asked how I would react if I knew of my father becoming involved in criminal activity again after becoming a police officer. I didn't hesitate to say that I would turn him in and make sure that justice was done. I wasn't going to let him ruin this opportunity in my life by showing any sympathy. The superintendent seemed pleased, and referred to me as a "self-made man." He applauded me for overcoming a past that included a family of criminals and despicable people. I took full credit for those words that he spoke to me that day, and patted myself on the back for reaching this place in my life.

A week later we concluded our training, and our graduating class consisted of 52 cadets. We were informed during the last week of training that unfortunately there were not enough openings in the department for all 52 of us, and approximately 15 to 20 of us were sent to the State Police posts nearest our home towns until our appointments. I was one of those who did not immediately receive my appointment. Although I had finished third in my class in physical training, my academic skills were not as good, and I was to report to the South Bend, Indiana post a week later, which was a week before Christmas. By the time I left the academy I felt almost invincible, something like Superman I suppose. I'm sure it's a common feeling for many young people who go through military school or police training. We prove ourselves and then come out gung ho, ready to save the world.

I took great pride in my accomplishment of making it through the training of the academy and graduation. At the time I considered it the greatest accomplishment of my life, and my mother was very proud of me. She followed my progress during the weeks I was at the academy, and I would often stop by to see her in Michigan when I was home on leave during the weekend breaks.

(40th Recruit Class Indiana State Police, Graduation photo December 1980, John third row down From top, second from left)

One of my roommates that graduated with me, Mike Rhymer, was from South Bend, and he invited me to stay at his home until my appointment. I gladly accepted, and appreciated the hospitality he and his wife showed me. Mike was a sort of hard-nosed guy, a former military policeman. He was tough, but had a tender and giving heart. He and his wife were Christians, and I felt very welcome in their home. Although I was not a Christian, they did not treat me any differently, and did not push their faith on me. I stayed with them for a couple of months, and then rented a place near the post. During that time Mike and I worked in the post together learning the various operations of the State Police. It was very helpful, but we were not yet sworn officers, and had no police powers, no badge or uniforms, and we still felt like cadets. We were anxious for the day we would receive news to report to Indianapolis.

The news came first for me the first week of April 1981. I was informed that my appointment was to the district headquarters in Evansville, Indiana. I had never heard of it. I only knew that it was in the deep southwest portion of the state, located across the Ohio

River, bordering on Kentucky, and just east of southern Illinois. I would first report to the State Capital in Indianapolis to be sworn in with five or six others who also received appointments.

(John, second from left, being sworn in by Chief Justice Givens of the Indiana Supreme Court)

I reported first to the State Police Headquarters in Indianapolis wearing a suit and tie. I met the other cadets I had graduated with and we were all hustled into a room. Moments later the Superintendent of the state police came in with a photographer who took photos as he congratulated us. Afterward we were escorted across the street to the state capital and were officially sworn in by Chief Justice of the Indiana Supreme Court, Judge Givens. Photos were taken while we were sworn in as state troopers and received our badges. Following the congratulations we reported to the state police quartermaster to receive our uniforms.

My friends knew that I came from a childhood that was pretty messed up, and that my father was in prison most of those years. They saw me as some kind of miracle kid for surviving my past and getting through school without becoming a problem kid with no future.

I had overcome a past that you rarely read about. My mother came from a traditional Roman Catholic background. Her father was a polish immigrant, and was very strict in her upbringing. She attended Catholic school, practiced all the traditions of the Catholic Church, but after meeting my father she was pregnant at age 16. My grandfather had planned on having her sent to a home for unwed mothers, but she ran away with my father to get married. For years after this my mother's relationship with her father was strained, and as a result we were effectively treated as if we did not exist. My mother tried to mend the strained relationship with her father by having me baptized Catholic and training me early on in the ways of the Catholic Church, but it did not last.

My father was a high school dropout. He was born in Detroit, Michigan and spent most of his life growing up on a farm with his family in Lowell. He had four brothers and four sisters and he loved animals. I knew little or nothing about his personal life as he grew older. I only knew that when he met my mother at the age of 18 he was a fast talker, good at making people laugh, and very handsome. It was the mid 1950's, and he loved working on cars, and was the kind of person who was very believable. He seemed to genuinely love my mother, but it was his nature to be very possessive, jealous, and controlling. My mother found out later that he was a womanizer and would pick a fight with anyone who tried to come between the two of them.

My father was a very violent man. During the early stages of his relationship with my mother he used threats of intimidation and physical abuse to control her. On one such occasion my mother later recalled to me that when she was five months pregnant, carrying me, and he beat her savagely after she had told him to leave her alone and stop teasing her. She was afraid that she would miscarry and lose me, but she survived. My mother actually left him shortly after this to live with her mother and father. My parents had not been married long, but my mother was already terrified of my father and the possibility of what could happen to her unborn child. She had to beg my grandfather to let her move in with them for awhile. Fortunately he allowed my mother to move home.

I was born in December just a few weeks after my mother turned 17, exactly one week before Christmas. On the night of my birth my grandmother Pearl was there with my mother. My father was not there. I learned years later that he was out with another woman, and this was the pattern of his marriage to my mother.

Within a few months of my birth my mother was stalked by my father. She started going to school again, trying to have somewhat of a normal life when he would show up in public places where she would be with friends. My mother denied knowing him, but he would seize the opportunity to humiliate her in front of her friends, telling everyone she was a married woman and the mother of his baby. My mother had gone back to school and concealed to her friends that she had a child. In 1956 the values and views of society were much different then, and because my father stalked my mother openly and humiliated her publicly she was afraid to have any kind of life. He would use this to control her and she eventually went back to living with him.

By May of 1957 my mother became pregnant again and when I was 14 months old my sister Mabel was born. Although my mother's father John (who I was named after) kept his distance from us, my grandmother Pearl loved us children deeply, and was so sweet to us. It was a struggle for my mother at such a young age to have two babies, and even though for years my grandfather remained distant, our grandmother treated us with love. It broke my mother's heart when our grandmother suddenly passed away in her sleep in July 1963, just a few months before President Kennedy was assassinated in Dallas. In addition, before I was five years old my mother suffered a miscarriage. After that there would be no more children, and life became more complex than ever.

Life as we knew it was never normal. It seemed like we would move every year or two. The beatings my father gave my mother were often, and we were terrified of him. It was typical for him to return home drunk late at night, and if my mother challenged him in any way on his whereabouts he shouted obscenities at her and beat her. There were times when my sister or I would upset him, and he would come after us. Our mother would always throw herself between us to stop him, and in the end he would take out his rage and anger on her. There were times when my mother moved us out of the home, taking us away when my father went to work, to get away from him. We would move in with an aunt or uncle, or any place we could take refuge. But he would find us, and threaten to kill my mother or harm us if we didn't return home with him.

My father worked and managed a shoe repair shop in downtown Grand Rapids when I was four years old. He was very skilled at working with his hands, and I remember him taking me to work with him, riding on the gas tank of his motorcycle. I would shine shoes for customers that would let me, although it must have been a scene to see a four year-old boy shining shoes. It was the summer of 1961 and I remember spending day after day with my father. My mother had taken a trip to California to visit an aunt, and I got to spend every day with my dad. In spite of the monster that my father was on most occasions, I was just a little boy in love with his dad, but that would all change as I became a pawn in my father's life. During that summer my father took me with him when he went to meet other women. I didn't understand at that age what was going on. Throughout my parent's marriage my father's infidelity would be the norm, along with the violence.

Life in our home was often filled with a sense of fear of my father. There was often tension in the air, and for a small child to even have any kind of normal life was only a dream. He was abusive and a tyrant. He would scream at all of us for different reasons that didn't matter, and often threaten us with physical violence. My sister was especially terrified of our father. There was a time when she actually got a fork stuck in her teeth and my father went into a rage, giving her a spanking that turned into a beating. My sister was only four years old. My mother was terrified and preparing to call the police when my father showed sorrow for his actions. As a result my mother never made the call, but my father never hurt my sister like that again.

The fights between my father and mother intensified because of his womanizing. He would lie no matter what, and there were times that his family members would become a part of the lie for him and provide an alibi. It was the pattern of life that existed for us.

I remember during those years as a child how I longed for loving attention from my father, in spite of the way he treated us. I had seen a side of him that was fun and daring. He liked to ride horses and had raised a few. He enjoyed finding horses at auctions that were wild, and he would buy them to break them and turn them into riding horses. He also liked to ride motorcycles and drive go-carts with super-charged engines.

I don't remember my father treating us kids with tenderness, or my mother. His affection for her seemed only physical at times. My mother constantly gave my sister and me love and attention. She was our protector and sacrifice when my father became a threat to us.

It was hard to have childhood friends for very long since we moved so much. I don't think I ever really knew what it was like to have a real relationship with a person. Maybe that's why my imaginary heroes were so important to me. I took them with me wherever I went. I remember living in my imagination as a small boy, thinking of my personal heroes like Superman and the Lone Ranger. Unlike most little boys who look to their fathers as their hero, mine were imaginary. I would only see my father as I hoped he could be; someone that I could one day win the love and approval of.

My father's family tree read like a chapter out of Charles Manson. His brother Peter Piper went to prison in 1966 for beating and raping a woman. Eventually he committed more horrible crimes (murder), and ended up in prison for life. Another brother, Herman, died of alcoholism. One of my father's sisters ended up as a heroin addict, murdered by her own husband, who was also an addict. Other members of the family spent time in jail or prison for various crimes. They were warped human beings. There were rumored incidents of incest in the family, and eventually my grandfather hung himself. As I grew older I detested having anything to do with these people. I considered them evil, and wanted nothing to do with them.

My parents divorced when I was eight years old. By then my father had a son by another woman he had been seeing for years. He was already about a year old. My mother raised me and my younger sister after leaving a marriage that had been characterized by a husband who was a womanizer, liar, thief, and violent. He terrorized us after the divorce, following us, threatening my mother with violence, verbal abuse, and stealing from us. He was the most self-serving man I ever knew. He would even steal the child-support checks out of our mailbox.

I was ten years old when my mother took my sister and me to Traverse City, Michigan to live. It was far enough away for my father to be less of a threat to us. My mother took a job caring for elderly people in an adult home to start, and later found work in a factory.

After moving away life seemed simple with the three of us. We were poor, but happy. My mother worked long hours to pay the rent, put food on the table, and clothes on our backs. She loved us dearly, and was grieved when she could not do more for us. There were times when we could barely get by, and I remember the powdered milk and government cheese. At Christmas when we couldn't afford gifts the Salvation Army and other charitable organizations reached out to us with food and gifts. We were so thankful with very little, and life was precious. We were together, and safe from my father.

There was no immediate family close to us, and all we had was each other. It was the late 60's and my mother began taking us to church. She was reaching out to find something more in life. She had left the Catholic Church a few years earlier and tried the Protestant Church, in particular the Pentecostal Church. My grandfather John had completely turned his back on us for giving up the Catholic faith, but my mother was searching for more. She seemed to have a belief in God, but was never committed or firm in her religion.

I remember my mother dating different men and living the life of a single mom. She was always very protective of us, and made it clear to the men in her life how much she loved us, and how important we were to her. She included my sister and me in times spent with her male friends, and it was apparent that we were a part of the package if she was going to ever marry again.

I missed having a father in my life. I never stopped loving my father, but at the same time a part of me grew to hate him. My friends sometimes asked about my father, and I would say he had died, or moved far away. I would say whatever came to my mind except for the truth. I was ashamed of telling anyone about my real father. In my heart I always loved him and desired a relationship with him, but it wasn't possible, and a part of me wanted nothing to do with him.

I continued to live in my imagination with my heroes. I often pretended as a young boy that I would someday save the world on my own. I never had a real hero in my life, and so I lived with them in my mind. They shaped my thinking and my attitude, and I hated anyone or anything that would hurt the innocent. I saw my father as the bad guy and every chance I got I would hurt someone who I thought represented him. I couldn't stand bullies in elementary school. I remember times when I not only stood up to them, but took my anger out on them with my fists. I got sent home once or twice for fighting, but I was determined to never let anyone hurt me or anyone close to me again. Like the time when I was nine years old. My younger sister came home crying because a bully from school named Dutch stole her bicycle. I knew who he was because of his reputation. He was my age and in my grade (4th). I went straight to his house and found him riding her bike on the street. I didn't ask any questions. I just knocked him to the ground, kicking and punching him until he was screaming and crying. He ran home and I took the bicycle home to my sister. He never touched my sister again. And the kids in school knew that I was no pushover or didn't take to threats.

I also began to take an interest in sports and music at a young age. I remember singing in elementary school and how it generated in me a peace that I had not experienced before. I liked singing with the choir. I had tried to learn playing a guitar at one time and a violin on another occasion, but they could not keep my interest. Singing was more enjoyable and it seemed to come naturally for me.

I grew and matured faster than most of the kids my age. I was naturally athletic and started playing sports in elementary school. I seemed to dominate most of the kids my age and became very competitive. I especially grew to love sports that involved physical contact like football. It gave me an opportunity to vent my frustration and anger that was inside me.

By the time I was age 12 my mother had found a father for us. His name was Russ. He had been a plant supervisor in a factory she worked at. They dated, and often he would take my sister and me with them for picnics. He made us feel like we were a true family. My sister and I fell in love with him. When our mother and Russ sat down to ask how we felt about them getting married we were excited. For the first time we thought we would truly have a normal life. A few months into the marriage we found out quite the opposite.

Russ quit his supervisor position at the factory and started his own business with another man. Within a short time his business partner took all the cash from their business and fled town, leaving Russ hanging out to dry and owing money to several people. His business failed. He was a perfectionist and he could not deal with the failure. He turned to drinking. As a result he became verbally abusive to my sister and me. In time it turned to physical violence against my mother.

To this day I will never forget the beating Russ inflicted on my mother one night. I was in my room upstairs in bed for the night, and my sister was asleep in the next room. I was awake, and could hear my mother and Russ arguing. She was pleading with him about his drinking, and then I heard the sounds of his fists crashing upon her face. I froze in my bed in terror, not able to move or speak out. The blows continued for some time, and my mother cried in pain. When it ended Russ realized what he had done, and he pleaded with my mother for her forgiveness. Somehow I drifted off to sleep.

The next day Russ was gone, and I saw the swollen face of my mother, black and blue. She tried to cover for Russ, telling me she tripped down a stairway and fell. I told her I knew the truth, and that I had heard it all. She told me to keep silent about it and not to tell my sister. She said it wasn't Russ's fault, and that he did not mean it, that it would never happen again. From that moment I hated him, and a part of me lost faith and trust in my mother for protecting this monster.

After that day I hid my feelings within myself and began my journey of self-destruction. I was still only 12 years old, but I soon grew up fast. I began to commit acts of juvenile delinquency, including my first burglary of a bicycle shop. I actually found the door of the business unlocked, but went in from the alley entrance, found money, which I stole, then left. I eventually broke the window of a nearby ice cream shop to steal again, and pull a neighborhood fire alarm on another night. The local fire department responded to my false alarm as I watched and hid nearby.

A couple of the local neighborhood boys that I associated with had previously been in trouble with the authorities, and when the police showed up to question them they pointed them in my direction. I ended up at the police station with my mother and my stepfather and confessed my crimes. Russ took the opportunity to tell me that I was just like my father and would not amount to anything.

What was odd to me was that the police officer who questioned me seemed to genuinely care about me. I remember him as Officer Benson. I had contact with him on more than one occasion because of my offenses and he took an interest in me. I started to look up to him as a role model, and in my mind I told myself that I wanted to be like him someday.

After I went to court and faced the juvenile judge I was placed on probation, and part of my restitution was to report to the local fire department for work that the fire chief assigned to me. It was the summer of 1969 when I met the local fire chief and he put me to work each morning painting fire hydrants. I don't remember the actual number, but it seemed like I must have painted every fire hydrant in Traverse City that summer.

Within a year my mother's second marriage was near an end. She packed up our things and took my sister and me back to Grand Rapids. I didn't want to leave. I had become attached to a small circle of friends and I didn't trust my mother. Although she had finally left her marriage with Russ I lost faith in her ability to choose what was best for us.

We moved in with some friends of my mother's. The first night we were there I slipped out of the house after everyone was asleep. I had taken my mother's car keys and rolled the car downhill out of the driveway in neutral. Somehow I managed to drive the car 150 miles back to Traverse City that night, parking behind a church where I fell asleep. I had no plan of where I would stay, or how I would live.

I was awakened early the next morning by a police officer standing over me. My mother was contacted and I was taken to the police station where they held me until she arrived with someone from Grand Rapids to take me back with her. There was no harm done to the car, and no charges were pressed, so the police were willing to let me go. All the way home I couldn't wait for the opportunity to run away again.

Within a week after our return to Grand Rapids I slipped out again after everyone was asleep. This time I had taken some money from one of my mother's friends and made my way to the local bus station, purchasing a bus ticket back to Traverse City. I took refuge in a shack living off the back of a house that belonged to a couple of kids my age. For two weeks I lived there, and again I committed another burglary of a business. I had gone into a department store, hiding inside until after closing, gathering merchandise in a wheel barrel, and carting it across town in the middle of the night. It was the next morning when a neighbor called the police because I had left the wheel barrel in their yard, and when the police came to investigate they recognized me standing outside next door.

I'll never forget that moment in time when I saw my mother at the police station after I was taken into custody and she came to Traverse City from Grand Rapids. I think it was the first time in my life that she slapped me in the face and told me what a disappointment I was. I don't know what I expected from her for a reaction, but perhaps I was hoping for some sympathy. By then the police had told her that the matter was out of their hands and I was taken to the juvenile home in Grand Rapids, otherwise known as the Kent County Juvenile Detention Center.

Chapter 2

I made the long trip to Evansville in April 1981 with another new trooper named Larry Rhodes. He was married, had lived in Indianapolis, and left his wife and baby there for awhile until he settled at our destination. We arrived at the post on a Sunday evening. The post commander, radio officer, and another trooper were at the post when we arrived. This was the district headquarters, and it was a new building, complete with training rooms, administrative offices, a holding cell, maintenance facilities for vehicles, and a barracks. We settled in for the evening, sharing a room at the barracks, which would be our home for the first few months.

The next day we reported to the first sergeant in charge of the district. Proudly displaying our new uniforms we were promptly told to change into work clothes, and for the first week or two we were assigned cleaning chores around the post. Our excitement quickly faded, and after we were reminded that we were rookies we were each assigned a training officer in different counties. For the next three months we worked in different counties that were a part of the Evansville district. Our training officers were seasoned officers who taught us everything they knew. We received training and instruction in the crime laboratory, with detectives, truck enforcement officers, and the majority would be on the job with experienced troopers. We worked shifts with them all week long, learning various aspects of traffic stops, investigating accidents, criminal investigations, handling drunk drivers, and various other responsibilities that were a part of the job. As police officers our training continued in other areas that included operations and certifications in radar and breathalyzer.

On Fridays Larry Rhodes and I headed north for the weekends. We would stop in Indianapolis at his home, and I would continue for another five hours north back to Grand Rapids. I would arrive late Friday nights. At the time I had been in a serious relationship with a girl for a couple of years, and now she was living with her parents. They had a room available for me at their home on weekends. I stayed there, and I visited family and other friends before leaving on Sundays to drive back to Evansville. This was a routine in my life for the next three months.

In July I learned that I would be primarily assigned to work in Vanderburgh County, which was the largest county in the area around Evansville. My fellow classmate Larry ended up assigned to Warrick County, which neighbored to the east of the county I was going to live and work in. Although these were our primary assigned areas we later often found ourselves working in adjoining counties when other officers might not be available. Our jurisdiction in the state extended everywhere, and we were quick to adapt to working rotating shifts that occasionally took us to neighboring counties.

Within a short period of time I was able to find an apartment to rent inside the Evansville city limits, and Larry found a home for his family in his assigned county. One of the great joys we had after getting our assignments to our perspective counties was when we received our own police cars. State police in Indiana at that time worked alone in their cars, and would drive them home, and off duty. It gave greater visibility to the state police, and made the department actually look bigger than it was. At that time in 1981 there were approximately 1200 state troopers.

Another officer took us to Indianapolis to pick up our vehicles at the state police quartermaster. Statistics showed that at least half of our graduating class would have accidents the first year, and we were all assigned used vehicles with 70,000 miles on them. To us it didn't matter because we finally had our own police cars, and it was a reward we had yearned for and finally received. Now that we had our training completed we were ready to finally work alone. I felt invincible, ready to save the world.

I'll never forget the first traffic citation I wrote. I was working the early morning shift and had witnessed a vehicle running a stop sign. I activated my overhead lights and the vehicle promptly pulled to the side of the road. After I approached the vehicle I asked the driver, a middle aged woman, for her license and registration. I explained the reason for pulling her over, and she politely gave me the documents. I was suddenly filled with stage fright, and started sweating profusely. I went back to my vehicle, running a check on her license and registration while she began to read a newspaper in her car, totally relaxed. I was like a nervous wreck, bumbling through my citation book, making sure everything was done correctly. I had done this several times with my training officers, but for some reason now it seemed like the very first time. Thankfully for me, even when I went back to the vehicle several minutes later to return her license, registration, and citation, she was cordial and polite. The rest of the day I spent driving around the county getting familiar with unknown roads. I had enough excitement for one day.

For the next two years I became very experienced and confident in my ability as an Indiana state trooper. I had received several commendations by the superintendent of the state police for arresting approximately 150 drunk drivers. I had also made many felony arrests, some that were most notable. I loved my job and was thrilled and excited about every opportunity to make an arrest. I was always eager to respond at any call for assistance or help and put the cuffs on any bad guys.

At that time the governor of the state was from Evansville. My superiors felt confident in my ability to protect the governor and provide for his services when he came into town from the state capital to stay at his private home, and sometimes to attend official events. The state police are responsible for the protection of the governor, and other troopers were assigned to protect him at all times when he traveled or was in Indianapolis. At least one officer would always be with his family at all times, and others would be close by. I picked him up at a private hanger at the airport when he arrived in Evansville and drove him to his personal residence or wherever he requested. I also took him to functions of his political party and stayed at his side continuously. I took great pride in the fact that I was often chosen to be the governor's bodyguard, and considered it an honor to serve him.

I also had the opportunity on at least one occasion to provide the same services as bodyguard for the lieutenant governor of the state when he came to Evansville on a later date for official reasons. He was very talkative when I picked him up, and appreciated the hard work and dedication of the department. A couple of weeks after I had the opportunity to serve him I received a personal letter of thanks.

During my first two years at the Evansville district I was involved in an incident that proved my value to the department, and I believe that it contributed to me being assigned to protect the governor on many occasions. I had been patrolling one evening with a truck enforcement officer who was riding with me. Another trooper had called for assistance as he pursued a vehicle westbound on Interstate 64. The vehicle was traveling at a very high rate of speed, in excess of 100 mile per hour. I was not far away and responded, as well as other units in the area. It was beginning to grow dark as I got onto the highway about a mile west of the last reported sighting. Not knowing why a vehicle was fleeing made me very cautious. I had managed to stop one vehicle on the highway that seemed to match the description of the fleeing car, but turned out to be an innocent driver. I got back in my squad car, and as other police cars passed by at a high rate of speed I noticed a faint light in my rearview mirror. It appeared to be just off the highway. I backed my car up quickly, about a quarter mile, and spotted a car that had just run off the highway. The engine was no longer running, but there was activity in the car. As I positioned my car and lights on the vehicle a man quickly exited on the driver side. I immediately identified myself as police and for him to stop, but he quickly bolted and jumped over a fence and started running north into a field. Instinctively I ran after him, jumping the fence and chasing him into the darkness. The truck enforcement officer immediately radioed other troopers for help who quickly responded to the area. As I chased the suspect through the field I drew my weapon and screamed at him to stop. I chased him about 300 yards when I caught him and tackled him. He tried to fight me but I had overpowered him and subdued him. Even after I had him handcuffed he continued to kick and try to fight. He seemed half crazed on drugs or something. I had to literally drag him toward the highway as several police cars were now on the scene and officers were calling out to me and flashing floodlights. After I yelled they spotted me and another trooper came out to help me drag the suspect back to the highway. After we got him back to the scene we pinned him on the ground while he continued to kick and fight.

A short time later we discovered the details of what had occurred. There inside the car was a woman who was the owner of the vehicle, and a young teenage boy who was related to the suspect. Apparently the woman had picked the two of them up in Ohio as they were hitchhiking, and the ride turned into abduction at knifepoint. The suspect had taken control of her car when they crossed into Indiana and was driving erratically and at a high rate of speed when he was spotted by another trooper. The suspect was also wanted in Ohio for parole violation. To make matters worse, when their engine failed and the suspect pulled off the highway he was in the process of sexually assaulting the victim when I drove my police car onto the scene. We also discovered that the suspect had a lengthy prison record that included convictions for rape. After that night he never saw freedom again. That incident gave me recognition with the older seasoned troopers, and respect.

(John receiving award from Superintendent John Shettle at Press Conference)

Some of the unpleasant experiences of the job involved investigations that involved traffic fatalities, aircraft accidents, and attending autopsies of people who had been murdered or killed in automobiles. The first time I attended the autopsy of a murder with another rookie officer we were told to undress the victim on the cutting table. Over a period of time seeing death, and witnessing terrible scenes that would make a normal person cringe became second nature to me. It was a part of my job to be around events of this type.

After I had been in Evansville for three years I put in for a transfer to the post in Granger, Indiana, which was the Indiana Toll Road. I had wanted to transfer north to live closer to my immediate family for some time. My goal was to eventually transfer to the South Bend post where I had been initially assigned after graduating from the academy. I had hoped to spend the rest of my career there and retire.

I should also mention that at that time in my life I never had personal relationships with women that lasted. Although I had been in a relationship with a girl from Michigan for about two years when I went to Indiana I was promiscuous. There was a part of me that cared about her, but at the same time I was selfish on the inside. Within a few months of our breakup I met a young woman from Evansville named Judy who was in the process of going through a divorce. Her life modeled that of my mother as a young woman because her husband had also battered her and terrorized her. She was a small petite woman and had two young sons, ages three and 12. I saw the fear she had been living in and I became fond of her. At the same time something welled up inside me, an anger and rage that is difficult to describe. I became her protector and within a short time of dating her I had her move in to my apartment with her two sons. Her divorce had become final and even though she was still afraid of her ex-husband he never threatened her or attempted to hurt her after she started dating me and was living with me. I never had to meet him face to face or talk to him. Somehow he was afraid of what I represented. He didn't know me, but the fact that I was a police officer was enough to keep Judy and her sons safe. I came to care about all of them deeply, and when I transferred north to the toll road they moved with me. We had talked about marriage, but I had never believed in marriage. I saw it as a failure after witnessing what my mother had gone through years before in her first two marriages.

I had achieved a great deal of success at the Evansville district, and managed to switch districts with another trooper at the toll road post who had wanted to transfer to Evansville, which was closer to his home town. It was the only way I was able to transfer north due to the fact that the South Bend post was a very difficult place to get transferred to.

The toll road district was not a popular post with many troopers, due to the fact that officers were assigned to patrol approximately 150 miles of highway extending from the Ohio to Illinois border. The job could become very monotonous and routine. The toll road was divided into four patrol zones, and I was assigned to cover zone two from South Bend to Valparaiso, which was just east of Gary. What I eventually found out was that this district was in fact one of the most hazardous and dangerous in the state. At that time in 1984 Gary, Indiana was said to have one of the highest murder rates in the nation.

I worked rotating shifts, beginning with midnights, then second shift, and finishing with two day shifts. We worked six days on and two off, and it was very taxing physically. Often I never felt fully rested, and the schedule wreaked havoc with my body's time clock.

It was easy for me to make the transition from Evansville to the toll road. There were no major adjustments, although in time I learned about the different county jails throughout the district, their procedures, and I became familiar with the different county courts and judges. Each county had different requirements for booking prisoners, handling drunk drivers, felons, and court hearings. Some courts required posting bond for traffic offenses involving out-of-state motorists, and others would not.

One of my former roommates from the academy, Mike Rhymer, was a great help to me making the transition to my new assignment. Mike had received his appointment at the toll road and was assigned to work the same zone with me. Our shifts often overlapped and we spent many days and nights working together. Mike became a very close friend to me, much like a brother.

The dangers of working the toll road occurred when least expected. The very first night I worked zone two, which was a midnight shift on a weekend, I had arrested a drunk driver just west of the post. He was also in possession of marijuana, and was in handcuffs, sitting in the front seat as I drove toward the post to administer a breathalyzer test. I witnessed another vehicle making an illegal u-turn on the highway, and thinking it was only a traffic violation I attempted to pull the vehicle over. The driver fled, and I ended up in a pursuit that lasted several miles and involved other departments. The pursuit ended after chasing the vehicle westbound in the eastbound traffic lanes. I had boxed the vehicle in from the front with a county officer following in the rear of the vehicle, and we managed to force the vehicle to come to a stop. I was able to quickly pull the driver from the car and subdue her in handcuffs in the middle of the highway. It turned out to be a mentally challenged young woman who was not licensed to drive a car, and who had run away from home late at night. It was a wonder that no one was killed.

The following Monday I was welcomed to the district by the lieutenant in charge of the post. He congratulated me on my arrests my first weekend after my transfer, and over a period of time we formed a bond of trust and friendship. As our friendship grew he often invited me to have lunch with him and he treated me with kindness.

Chapter 3

Running away had been the pattern for me until I was taken to the juvenile home at age 13. I didn't know what it was like to be able to face something when there was adversity, and then somehow overcome it. When my mother saw me that last time before I was taken to the Kent County Juvenile Home she was very hurt by my actions. She had done so much to protect me already, and yet she could not understand now why I had turned into such a rebellious and uncontrollable person. When she slapped me in the face at the police station, she said to me, "You're no son of mine John Piper." At that time my legal name was John Joseph Piper, and to be associated with the family name of my father had notoriety. I had come from a family of people who had become known in the Grand Rapids area because of the criminal reputation of the family, and now it was as if I had somehow become one of them. My mother realized in her anguish what she had done, and told me she didn't mean what she said, but all I could remember were those words.

At that time in my life my father had been in prison for just over a year. I did not communicate with him, or see him until at least five years later after his release. But during those years my life went through many profound changes.

At the juvenile home I was assigned to a probation officer named Ken VanWoerkom. He was a young case worker who recently graduated from Calvin College in Grand Rapids, Michigan, which is a Christian college. He was a very soft-spoken man, who seemed to care about my welfare. He spoke kindly to me many times, and tried to convince me that going back home with my mother would be the best thing for me. But I refused and continued to tell him that if I was sent home with my mother I would run away again.

After I had been at the juvenile home for a few months it was determined that the best thing for me would be to go to live in a foster home for awhile. This would hopefully help me adjust to life again, and the intention was to gradually re-establish a relationship with my mother. Once that was accomplished I could move back home with her and my sister.

A young couple, age 26, had inquired with the court about becoming foster parents, and had met me in person a couple of times at the juvenile home to see if we might be compatible for each other. My probation officer had arranged it, and it was determined that I would leave the detention center for a couple of weekends to spend with them and get to know them better. During those weekends the time spent together went very well, and it was determined by the court that I was to go live with them, and in six to 12 months the court would reconvene to examine my progress and determine my future.

My foster father was a high school English teacher, and my foster mother was an office manager for an employment agency. I remember that during the first month or so living with them I had pondered the thought of running away again. But these people really cared about me and I could see it. Somehow I became attached to them, and in time I would grow to love and respect them very much. Both of them were educated, caring, and very outgoing, and they exposed me to many things in life I had never experienced. Life at home with them was not what I had grown up with. There was no screaming and intimidation, no verbal abuse, and no fear of physical threats that I experienced when my father was around.

My foster father Mark was very athletic, had played sports in high school and college, and immediately helped me get involved playing rocket football when I went to live with them in the fall of that year. I was in junior high school, the eighth grade. He took me to practices after school days, and on weekends he took me hunting and fishing, which were things that I had never done with my father.

His wife Patricia was very supportive as well, and every time I had a football game they were there to watch and celebrate with me. They encouraged me in school academically, and challenged me to be the best that I could be, and took interest in everything I did.

I had never received attention like this before from an adult male, and Mark was like a combination between a big brother and a father. He taught me so many things, like snow skiing, how to swing a golf club, play tennis, play pool, and throw a hook with a bowling ball. Mark and Pat took me water skiing with their family for the first time, and exposed me to so many wonderful things in life. The first year I lived with them I excelled in everything, and they never tried to force me to choose what they wanted for me. They gave me a choice. They encouraged me in everything I did.

My probation officer had arranged for me to begin spending occasional Saturdays or Sundays with my mother after I had been living with my foster parents for several months. These took place maybe once a month. I resisted going home to live with her. My mother was aware of the progress that was being made in my life with my foster family, and she became unselfish about her desires to have me home with her. It was a sacrifice she continued to make throughout my high school years.

Something had changed in my mother. She had come to a cross-road in her life where she had totally committed her life to God and become a born-again Christian. She had on previous attempts in her life never made a total commitment, but I began to recognize something inside her that I had never seen before. From that time on my love and respect for my mother grew.

By the time I was 15 years old it was determined by the court, and agreed upon by my mother, that my progress with my foster parents was so great, that I should continue to live with them indefinitely. It was what I wanted, and my mother continued to sacrifice her personal feelings for my welfare. I continued to be a ward of the court for another year or so, and my juvenile record was eventually expunged due to the fact that there were no further incidents of delinquency in my life. My probation officer, Ken VanWoerkom, took a great deal of interest in my progress during this time, and he also had become a friend to me. He saw me as a success story of a kid from a broken home that had overcome adversity and became something.

My high school years were spent at Lowell High School in Lowell, Michigan. My foster father Mark taught at this school. We made it a point that I would not attend any classes he taught so that there would not be any undue pressure on either of us. He had always encouraged me to be the best I could be at everything I did, and somehow I did not feel comfortable with the idea of sitting in his classroom.

These were some of the best times of my life. I led a busy life, playing sports year round, singing in choir and musicals, living a life that brought me many new experiences. My foster parents were always present at sporting events I was in, and when the choir performed concerts, they were there for me. I fell in love with the game of football, and my foster father Mark always gave me praise, win or lose, after a tough game. Both my foster parents took me to college football games at their alma mater, Central Michigan University. They had also instilled in me the importance of education on my future, and they were instrumental in my decision to go to college after high school.

During my high school years my mother was there for me too, coming to all my games, my concerts, musicals, and plays. She never interfered in my life, and silently watched me grow. Sometimes she invited me out afterwards, and sometimes I would say yes. Most of the time I had plans with my friends, and I realize now that it broke her heart many times when she left to return home without her son.

When I spent time with my mother while I was in high school it was never very long, but as I grew older that time together grew. I witnessed in her the profound changes that God had made in her life. I recall going to church with my mother, out of love and respect. I believed in God, that he had a son named Jesus Christ, and that he had died on a cross, but I never made a commitment to live for him, and I didn't ask him to come into my heart. My mother had spoken to me many times about the love of Christ, and how He died for me, but pretending to be the attentive son I would listen for awhile, and then go off to do my own thing. Many times when I went with my mother to church I could never understand how all those people were weeping and raising their hands to God. My mind was always somewhere else, and I couldn't wait for services to end so I could leave to pursue my own personal desires.

My foster parents were not religious people, did not attend church, and I had never been to a church with them, except to attend a wedding or a funeral. We never discussed it during the years I lived with them, and I would never learn what their views were about Christianity. They were good people, always taught me to do the right thing, but they never went to church.

It was during my high school years that my mother's relationship with her father John was restored. He had returned to his native country Poland in 1964, a year after my grandmother's death, and had married a polish woman named Nina. My grandfather brought her back to the United States to live. She spoke no English at that time, and did not know how to drive an automobile. During the years to follow she would speak broken English with a thick polish accent, and eventually my mother taught her many things. After several years my grandfather's heart softened and his relationship with my mother was restored. Our grandmother Nina became a second mother to her, and precious to all of us.

A year before I graduated from high school my father got out of prison. I had my own car, and I often drove to visit him in Grand Rapids where he lived. He had remarried years earlier, and his wife Carol gave him five more children, which included four sons and a daughter. Carol stayed married to him through his imprisonment, and he always returned home to her and the kids after his release. I don't know if life for them had been similar to what I experienced growing up. I know that the two oldest sons Ben and Randy were gifted working on cars like our father. I had a good relationship with them when I came to visit, which wasn't often. Our only connection during those years was when I came to their home. I never knew if they lived with the same terror I had experienced with our father, and I never asked.

Before graduating from high school I looked at several colleges and universities. I never lost my dream to become a police officer, and I wanted to attend a school that offered a degree in Criminal Justice. My goal was to become state trooper because I wanted to be a part of the best department in the state. I had considered Central Michigan University where my foster parents had gone to school, but the university did not have a degree program in Criminal Justice. Instead I chose to attend Grand Valley State College in Allendale, Michigan, which was at that time a small division II school. Years later it grew and became a university. My plan was to attend Grand Valley to pursue my career, and also to play football.

Just before I graduated from Lowell my foster parents Mark and Pat sat down to tell me they were getting divorced. I was totally shocked and devastated. I could not understand how this could happen. They were quick to assure me that it had nothing to do with me. When school ended and I went off to take a summer job Mark and Pat separated, with Mark taking possession of the house and Pat moving into an apartment. I still had a home to come to, but things were never the same. In time I lost all contact with Pat, and my relationship with Mark drifted farther away as he remarried and I went off to college.

When I graduated from high school in June of 1975 my mother proudly held an open house to celebrate, and many family and friends attended. This was in many ways the beginning of permanently reconnecting with my mother and sister and other relatives. All of my holidays while going to college would now be spent with them, since my foster family had disintegrated.

Throughout high school and heading off to college music became very important to me through singing in choir and taking parts in musicals. It was a way for me to express myself. I rarely got emotional or passionate about anything except for singing and acting. It brought out a part of me on the surface that is difficult to describe. I guess that since I often buried my feelings it was a way to bring them out. It was through this medium in my life that I had some very good relationships with teachers and classmates.

My high school choir teacher invested much time with me giving me instruction in studying voice, taking parts in musicals, and he often gave me opportunities and encouraged me to use this gift in my life. It was something I loved to do, and it gave me a confidence in myself that helped me develop a good side of my personality that people might not have ever seen.

When I went to college my freshman year I lacked confidence in myself for awhile to get involved in singing, except for studying voice with Leslie Eitzen, who I mentioned earlier. She had a successful career many years earlier in the New York Metropolitan Opera as a mezzo soprano, a female voice similar in range to a soprano, but with a darker color and the ability to extend the range lower. I met with her each week to train in singing, and during that year she encouraged me to audition for the GVSU singers, an elite group of college singers led by another professor in music, William Beidler.

After the audition I was invited to join the GVSU singers, a group of about 20 college singers. William Beider had developed this group throughout the year to perform in musicals, pops concerts, and even opera. In the spring of each year the group toured schools and churches throughout the state to perform what was called Swingout. It was a combination of Broadway music performed with dance.

The GVSU singers became a second family to me. In the fall of my sophomore year the entire group spent a weekend at Blue Lake Fine Arts Camp to begin exercises in singing and dance and prepare for the upcoming year. This was a yearly occurrence for the group to get acquainted and rehearse. When regular classes began I continued to study voice with Leslie Eitzen once a week while rehearsing and singing with the GVSU singers five days a week.

William Beidler, or Mr. B as we affectionately called him, was very passionate about music. Those of us who sang for him became more than students. We were like adopted children. To this day I've referred to myself as his adopted son to others when asked if I was his son.

The GVSU singers met every day for rehearsals during the school year and we became a very tight-knit group. It was the best part of my life in college. The other singers became my close friends and I think most of us looked at B as a father figure.

Even after graduating and leaving Grand Valley the impact of music in my life continued to inspire my love for theatre, musicals, and opera. And my friendship with William Beidler continued for years. I have loved him like a father and it has been a privilege to know him.

While going to college I continued to follow my passions for football and music. I was only an average student, not totally committed to studying. I realized quickly that if I didn't maintain decent grades I would not be able to continue my education. I buckled down and did enough to get by. My love of football always remained, but after two seasons I found that it wasn't as exciting in my life as it once was. My focus intensified on a career in law enforcement, and by the time I was 20 I had an opportunity to get a part-time job as a child care worker at the juvenile home where I had once been held seven years earlier in my life. When I had interviewed for the job I had the support and backing of my former probation officer Ken VanWoerkom. He had a great deal of confidence in me, and thought that I would be able to relate to the teens there due to my background.

Still in college, I was hired to work at the Kent County Juvenile Home in August 1977. Many people who had known of my past, including my mother, displayed a great deal of pride in me for the accomplishments I had made, and for the next three years I gained a great deal of experience working there with troubled teens while completing my degree at Grand Valley.

My relationship with my father changed very little. I would see him now and then, but we were never close. I had always yearned for his attention, hoping one day to make him proud of me. If I could ever gain his approval it would make my life complete. But he was a very hard man, mostly motivated by greed and his own interests. The pattern of his life was to contact me only when he wanted something.

By October of 1979 my father dropped out of my life again and as he was sent back to prison for another crime. A part of me wanted to forget about his existence, as if he had never lived. My heart was always torn about my feelings for him. Half of me loved him, and yet another part of me hated him, and I always told myself I would never ever be like him.

Everything I had worked so hard to accomplish finally culminated in my new career with the Indiana State Police. Many people who knew of my painful past heaped praises on me for my success. I was very disciplined in my life to follow my personal desires to achieve whatever goal I put in front of me, and I took full credit for every gift I possessed, but my mother always praised God for every blessing, and she often talked to me to emphasize that everything came from Him.

Chapter 4

There were times when I had come out unscathed from some close calls while on duty. On one particular late Friday night I had been working zone one of the toll road, which covers the area extending from Valparaiso to the Illinois state line. I had stopped a drunk driver on the eastbound portion of the road at mile marker nine, just west of Gary. I was outside my car with the driver, between both vehicles, and on the side of the road, when suddenly without warning a loud noise that sounded like a roaring train occurred. The driver and I were both showered with glass from my car. A semi had side-swiped my patrol car, breaking windows and destroying the driver's door. The driver continued down the road at a high rate of speed. Shaken, I called for assistance on my radio, but the nearest Trooper was sixty miles away. It was fortunate that neither I nor the driver were injured or killed.

On another occasion I had been working late at night, just before midnight, responding to assist another trooper at an accident. A semi driver had fallen asleep at the wheel and gone off the road into the median. His trailer side-swiped a concrete overpass and tore the side off completely. The trailer was loaded with stereo equipment, which now covered the highway. This was a rural area, and soon some vehicles stopped on the overpass to observe what was going on. As I arrived some of the observers had come down off the overpass and were in the process of looting the accident scene. Another officer was on the scene and had one looter in custody in his vehicle. The other looters dropped the merchandise and fled back up the hill with me chasing them on foot. At least two vehicles had already driven off. I managed to reach the top of the hill when a third vehicle, a pickup truck, was just leaving the scene, but coming in my direction. Standing in the middle of the road facing the oncoming truck I had ordered the driver to stop, but he accelerated with the intention to run me over. Without thinking I instinctively moved quickly to avoid being struck, and as the driver passed by me I drew my weapon and began firing, first shooting out a rear tire, then emptying my gun into the rear of the cab. Within minutes other officers responded to the scene after hearing a broadcast of the events that an attempt had been made on the life of a fellow officer. I was quite shaken, but my body was pumped with adrenaline, and within two hours officers located the vehicle and the perpetrator at a rural farmhouse. He had taken refuge in a neighboring barn. When I arrived with other troopers the barn was surrounded. A tactical team eventually went into the barn when he refused to come out and took him into custody without firing a shot.

Whenever these or similar incidents took place in my life I always took personal credit for coming out of it without injury. There had been times when I could have been seriously hurt or killed, and in my arrogance I always patted myself on the back, as if I was some kind of Lone Ranger. It was almost as if I had become the hero I had imagined as a small boy growing up.

I rarely had contact with my father most of my career as a state trooper. He had been paroled from prison after his second trip, and in 1982 he committed another felony before his discharge from parole. He appeared in my life again in late 1984 after being released on parole. He seemed to take great pride in the fact that I was a police officer, and yet he hated what I represented. He respected me, and although I still loved him, I never trusted him. Our relationship never seemed to form a common bond of love and trust.

In 1985 my career and my life took a turn that I had never planned or expected. I had been at the toll road district two years and was steadily becoming disgruntled and unhappy. My friend and former academy roommate Mike had resigned and chosen another career for several reasons which included low pay and dissatisfaction with the job. I was finding that several aspects of the job were political, and at least one person who outranked me had put pressure on me more than once because they did not feel that I was performing my job according to their expectations. I began to resent this, and as time went on my attitude towards my job began to change.

I began to question my purpose as a state trooper, and whether I was really making a difference in the world. My heart began to harden, and it's hard to explain why, but I increasingly resented any authority over me, and I considered that perhaps my future might be more rewarding if I set a new goal to do something bigger and better. I took the written exam for the Federal Bureau of Investigation (FBI), and had also made an inquiry with the U.S. Secret Service. My pursuit of these possible career changes did not go anywhere.

I started to treat the job that I once loved as a burden, and I began to drink a lot. I seemed to have a well of anger in me that continued to grow. Within several months I turned against everything I represented and had believed in. It began when I started to take money that had been intended to go to one of the local county courts. One of the counties that I patrolled was LaPorte County, and the county seat was located in Michigan City. The judge who presided over traffic cases required that police seize driver's licenses for out-of-state motorists as bond for any traffic offenses. Traffic violators had the option to post a cash bond, or sign off on the traffic citation to plead guilty to the violation, and pay the fine. They were required to pay cash, and it was my responsibility to escort them to the nearest postal mailbox to deposit the cash. In my arrogance I began to see this as a burden for me, since I usually had to escort someone several miles to a mailbox located off of the toll road, and truck drivers who were usually pressed for time did not want to have to lose more time. Often they requested that I mail the signed ticket and cash for them, and I began at first to do this. But as my attitude toward my job changed so did my thinking. I started collecting envelopes and never mailing them. I later opened them, counted up the cash, and destroyed the tickets, except for a copy I would turn in to the department for records. In the end it was my undoing. I justified my actions to myself, thinking that guilty traffic violators were getting what they deserved, and it wasn't hurting anyone if I kept some of the proceeds now and then and put it in my own pocket. The way I did this was quite reckless, because if I had been planning this I would have used bogus ticket books that could not be traced back to me, and I would never have turned in any records of making a traffic arrest. I could have simply destroyed any and all records of any kind, and been able to continue stealing without knowledge by anyone but myself.

My bending the rules and the law changed many things about me. It escalated to taking drugs from people and not arresting them. I primarily seized marijuana and took it for my own use. I used it habitually with alcohol in my off-duty hours to escape from the world and the responsibilities I had taken for granted. It was as if a part of me was re-writing the very laws I was supposed to enforce, and I was becoming more of a recluse on the job and in my private life. I pretended everything was alright on the outside when in reality there was something going on inside of me that I could not understand and didn't know how to deal with.

My mother had come to visit in South Bend on many occasions, and for some time all seemed well before I began drinking, drugging, and stealing. For those first two years after the transfer I took my job seriously and went about doing my work with a sense of pride and dignity. My mother had often encouraged me to get involved with a local church, and one time I went to visit a local church with Judy, but I felt out of place. I had no sense of God because I had never lived for Him. I could not comprehend what it would be like to live for any other purpose than my own.

Judy, who I had mentioned earlier, was the girlfriend from Evansville that I had been living with in South Bend. She knew something was going on with me when I came home from the job after stealing bond money. When we first moved to South Bend after the transfer I was a protector and provider for her. I know she was confused and could not understand the drinking and drugging I was doing after we were in South Bend for over two years. Her oldest son Mark had moved away to live with his father and the youngest son Jeffrey was only about five years old and too young to grasp what was going on.

By February of 1986 I had been pocketing bond money for about six months, and continuing to seize marijuana from suspects that I would have otherwise arrested. I continued to feed my habit of excessive drinking and drugging when not working, and my judgment, work ethic, and professional demeanor slowly vanished. I became the "bad cop" you see in movies who would take a drug suspect's money and drugs, then tell them to get lost. They would never argue or question, because if they did they knew they would go to jail.

Somehow I saw a glimmer of what I had become, and I thought if I was able to transfer to another district I could rid myself of this person. I had been attempting to transfer from the Toll Road District to the Bremen District, formerly the South Bend District, and was finally successful in getting it approved. By March 1st my transfer to Bremen was effective, and I was finally leaving the toll road. I thought I would get a new start, no longer pocket any traffic citation proceeds, and somehow return to honesty and integrity. But it never happened.

The last week of February, before my transfer, I filled my pockets with several envelopes of cash from out-of-state traffic offenders. One of those offenders was a bus driver for Greyhound Bus Lines out of Chicago. The irony of what happened is that this was the last person I would ever take money from.

A few weeks after my transfer I received a telephone call from the district executive officer at the toll road. He advised me that the bus driver had called the post inquiring about a receipt he never received for paying his traffic ticket. I pretended to not know who he was talking about, since it was not uncommon to make hundreds of traffic arrests during the year. Apparently they had traced the record I had turned in of the arrest, so they knew that I was in fact the officer who was involved.

By the end of March my world turned upside down and the imaginary glass house I lived in as a police officer was shattered. I received an official letter through channels of an internal investigation regarding possible misconduct. I began to plan a way out of my situation by creating a series of lies that only lead to more lies. One fateful day I had left my house early in the morning to go to the Bremen district after notifying the radio operator that I was in service (on duty). On my way to the post I was contacted by radio and advised to report to the district commander at the toll road. I knew what it was about, and advised that I was enroute to one of the local county courts for a hearing. I was immediately advised to notify the court of a schedule conflict, and advised that the district commander was ordering me to report. I acknowledged the radio operator, and instead of driving to the post I drove my squad car home quickly, and in a panic. I told Judy to call the post and tell them that I had gone to one of the medic centers due to illness. She had no idea what was going on but she was afraid for me and she made the call. In the meantime I made a call to the state police headquarters in Indianapolis and requested a loan of my pension, which was approved and released to me that same day. It was as if I was plotting my escape. I got in my state police car and drove to Indianapolis to pick up a cashier's check for about $2500. While all this was happening the state police in the district I lived in began to search the city for me. Officers converged on my home and neighborhood, and checked all medical centers in South Bend, only to find that I had never gone to any of them. The state police also took advantage of air support to use a helicopter to search the area for me.

By late afternoon I had made my way back to South Bend. The department had thought that perhaps I had gone back to the Evansville district and placed an all points bulletin regarding my whereabouts. Somehow I had managed to elude them, but coming back into town I was soon spotted. I parked my car in my garage at home, changed clothing, and fled from the house with my pistol and badge, with no plan, no destination in my mind, and fear closing in on me on every side. I had seen the helicopter hovering over the neighborhood in search of me, and I managed to find my way to a nearby tavern. I stayed there drinking until late at night, then crept back to my home. I found that the district captain came to my home with a detective, confiscating all of my uniforms, my car, and weapons. He had left his home phone number with Judy.

At 2:00 a.m. I placed a call to his home to tell him I was ready to talk and tell them everything. I was in fact ready to confess everything, and planned to meet the district headquarters captain and lieutenant at the toll road district in an hour. I also made a phone call to my friend and former academy roommate Mike.

I confessed all to him, and considering my best interest Mike advised me to contact an attorney before telling everything I knew to the state police captain. Even when I told Mike all those things I don't think he even understood, and maybe he questioned if he ever even knew me.

Mike picked me up to take me to the post and waited outside while I went in for questioning. Those present included the district area headquarters captain, the district lieutenant who knew me personally, and a detective assigned to the investigation. The captain read my Miranda Right to remain silent, and he also advised me of the administrative policies of the state police, which basically stated that I had no rights, and according to the policies, I was required to answer all questions truthfully whether I had committed criminal offenses. I stated that I wanted to consult an attorney before waiving any rights at that time, and the captain gave me 24 hours to make a decision.

I didn't sleep that night after leaving. I knew that my life and career as a police officer was over as I had known it. By morning I had contacted an attorney and made an appointment. I also contacted my mother in Michigan. I found that they had contacted her earlier the previous day when searching for me, and she had been in tears and fearful of what had happened to me. I lied to my mother and concocted a story to make it look as though the department had the wrong man. In her heart I think she knew I was guilty, but she stood by me to provide her love and support.

When I met the attorney the next morning I told him the details of my guilt, and seeing that all the charges against me were completely circumstantial he advised me to resign my position with the Indiana State Police. He composed a letter that day addressed to the district area captain, informing him that he was representing me, and that the police were not to question me without his presence. A letter of my resignation with my signature also contained his signature.

Within 24 hours my life became a nightmare as the state police released the story to the local news media. Local television and radio somehow had received my unlisted phone number and began calling my home for interviews. I witnessed the local news on television reporting the investigation, and my entire life was visible to everyone in the community, including my neighbors, and any friends that I had.

By evening I had rented a moving truck, loaded it with all the furniture in the house, and fled the city to southern Indiana to stay with some friends who lived in a remote area. Judy went with me, along with her youngest son, and we temporarily resided there until we found a house for her to live in.

I learned that soon after my departure from South Bend the prosecutor in LaPorte County had issued warrants for my arrest charging me with Felony Theft and Official Misconduct. They had notified the authorities in Michigan, thinking I had moved back to my home town. For about a week I was afraid to return or even contact my attorney. When I finally called him he convinced me to return and turn myself in with him for arraignment and arrest.

It was arranged and I met my attorney at his office in South Bend. My mother came from Michigan to provide bond money for me. I know it broke her heart to see me standing before a judge and prosecutor I had once worked with, now in front of them as the person being charged. After arraignment my bond was posted, and it was agreed that I would accompany my attorney to the county jail to be fingerprinted and have my picture taken. I did not know the two state police detectives who did the fingerprinting and picture taking, but it was humiliating for me. I had the feeling that what was happening was not real, but in fact it was.

For the next several months my life came to a standstill as I waited for a trial. My attorney made the case for the prosecutor very difficult, as he had the county clerk's office audited for all money received for traffic offenses. The audit revealed several funds that were missing from other sources besides me. That evidence alone put holes in the prosecutor's case against me.

I could not find a regular job and had lost purpose. I had lived all my life knowing exactly what I wanted and what I was going to become, until now. There was nowhere to go, and nothing I could do. I had always been the one in control of my destiny, and now I had no plan. I could not turn back the clock and right all the wrongs

I had done. I would not accept any blame. How could they do this to me, after all the good I had done? How could they take away my career after all the awards, commendations, and after all the bad guys I had locked away. I was full of pride, and refused to take responsibility for my actions.

The anger and rage that swelled up inside of me made me want to get even with the system that I had at one time represented with dignity and respect. As a result I took the skills I had learned as a police officer and began to commit burglaries. Specifically, I targeted businesses like shopping centers and taverns that kept large amounts of cash on hand on weekend nights. The money was always locked in safes, and I had learned about safe-breaking techniques that criminals used. I began to use these techniques to develop my own skills for safe-breaking. As a result I came away with large amounts of cash. I used the money to buy more drugs, alcohol, and even to pay my attorney more money when he requested it. By now I was using cocaine and spending more money.

I became very sophisticated in my planning and execution of committing these burglaries. I always "cased" the business before staging the actual crime. Often I entered the businesses during regular hours posing as a customer so I could examine the layout of the store or tavern, looking for alarm systems, the location of the office where money was usually located, and any other information that would be of help to me. If the opportunity was there I would stroll by the office to get a quick look at the safe. I also observed the business at closing to check the routine of the owner(s) and employees, whether they carried deposit bags from the business, or stayed late.

My plans would always include an alternative plan in case something unexpected happened, like the police or someone showing up. I preferred to target businesses that were located in rural areas or small towns that did not have a local police department. My intent was to get in, commit the burglary, and escape quickly without being detected.

I usually carried a back pack with my tools to leave my hands free. Sometimes I had to scale fences or walls, and having the ability to move quickly was a necessity. I would plan every part of the burglary, and treat it like a mission. My entrance and exit was part of my strategy, and even how I dressed. I had special clothing for the job in the trunk of my car along with my tools, and I always found a place to park quite some distance from the intended target where my vehicle would not look out of place. If there was a nearby apartment complex I might park there, or if possible I parked off the road in a wooded area where vehicles did not normally travel.

I carried a portable police scanner with an earpiece to monitor the channels of the departments that might be in the area. I also carried a handgun, a .38 caliber Smith and Wesson revolver I owned and used as a backup weapon when I was with the State Police. In my mind I never envisioned that I would use a gun, but I felt safer knowing it was on my person. I always wore gloves and a dark hooded mask. Just in case I was spotted accidentally I did not want to be identifiable.

Armed with the tools, knowledge, and planning, I developed and improved my skills with every burglary. I even began to time myself, and determine that with each business I burglarized I would only take so much time to accomplish the mission set before me. In my mind I had begun to develop a satisfaction that I was getting back at the system that had turned against me and ruined my life.

I think Judy was relieved that I had moved her back to southern Indiana. Her oldest son had moved back home with her and the youngest son after their father died of alcoholism. Judy was staying with relatives now who cared for her and the boys until she could find a place of her own. Her former husband was no longer a threat to her, even with me out of the way.

If I ever had a conscience I don't know where it was during the crime spree I was on. My heart had become so hardened to everything that had taken place, and each day I lived like an escapee looking over my shoulder. I didn't trust anyone, and when I wasn't preparing to commit a burglary my only objective was to get high and stay that way.

I was traveling back and forth to Indiana after committing burglaries in Michigan. I would go to see Judy and her sons, but my mind was always somewhere else, wondering about the next job I would pull. For a few years before everything happened I had played house, so to speak, but never committing myself to anything permanent. It was convenient for me and I never believed in marriage anyway. For Judy I know it was security and protection from her former husband.

I had returned to Michigan and was living with a friend I grew up with in high school. He was single and worked midnights, which was convenient for me because that was the time I would commit my crimes. By now I was also using more cocaine, in addition to drinking every night and smoking marijuana daily. Every day I wanted to escape from reality. There were times when I also considered taking the .38 caliber revolver I had, sticking it in my mouth, and pulling the trigger. I was living one day at a time, not caring if tomorrow would ever come.

My crime spree had been going on about nine months, until the night of March 4, 1987. It had been 11 months since I resigned from the Indiana State Police and I was still free on bond from the charges brought against me back in LaPorte County. On this particular night I had targeted a shopping center in Byron Center, which is a small town located south of the city of Grand Rapids. It was a late Sunday night, and I had managed to gain entrance into the business through a freezer door located in the rear of the building. I was able to secure the door from the inside so that it was secure. I quickly moved to the front of the store and entered an office area located up a short staircase. Within moments I heard voices and saw flashlights. What I didn't know was that a county deputy from the sheriff's department was checking doors in the back of the building and found an unlocked door that a store employee forgot to lock at closing. I had gotten careless that night, failing to carry my police scanner. The officer had called for backup, and within moments he and another deputy were facing me with flashlights and guns drawn. I was also armed with my .38 handgun, which was holstered. They ordered me against a wall, and as I moved toward the wall I charged and crashed into both deputies. The three of us went tumbling down the stairway behind them, and I attempted to get up and run as one of the officers grabbed onto one of my legs. Within moments a third officer on the scene tackled me, and I was finally subdued and handcuffed. Soon other officers showed up, including the shift supervisor Larry

Stelma. After I was photographed I was placed in a police car and taken to the Kent County Jail.

When I was finally arrested in Michigan all I could think of was escape. No one knew who I was at the time, and somehow I thought that if I managed to escape they would never find out and I would be free. I was not living in reality, and it was as if time was suddenly standing still. Every minute of the day and night my mind was racing, and my heart was pounding.

Even after my capture I wanted to escape. I contemplated suicide. More than anything I wanted it all to end. The authorities wanted to know if I would be trying to kill myself and I had to convince them that it would never happen and that I was not considering it, which was another lie. It was all I could think about for a long time. I devised many times in my mind how I would do it, but if I had gone through with it I wanted to be certain that it would only take one attempt and I would be successful.

I think I was close to losing my grip on reality because everything that had happened, even before I was finally arrested in Michigan, seemed like a movie playing over and over in my head. My mother had never confronted me about my guilt or innocence when I appeared the year before in an Indiana courtroom on the charges of Felony Theft and Official Misconduct. She must have known in her heart that my denial was so strong that I would have lied to anyone regarding the truth.

She must have known how my mind was working. She was so devastated that she did not come to see me in the county jail. Instead my step-father Larry came to see me. He pleaded with me not to hurt myself because it would heap even more pain on my mother. I couldn't comprehend the devastation I had already put them through, but somehow I knew in my heart that I could not go through with the suicide and put my family through something worse. In the back of my mind I also remembered what I had learned going to church with my mother, and somehow I realized that if I had taken my own life I would be separated from her forever and spend eternity in a place where I would be tormented.

I was booked into the jail under a false name I had given, Jack Summer. After I was fingerprinted and photographed again I was placed in a holding cell until two detectives named Orange and Miedema brought me out to question me early in the morning. I had refused to waive my Miranda Rights, and almost all of the information I gave them was false, including my home address. The detectives escorted me in handcuffs to the county courthouse in downtown Grand Rapids for formal arraignment, and they did not yet know my true identity. Before the hearing began they took me into a jury room located off of a hallway behind several courtrooms, and as soon as one of the detectives removed the handcuffs I bolted to the door and ran down the hallway. Both officers were chasing me, yelling, and I made a turn through the back door of a courtroom that was in session. Running past the clerk I jumped the railing in front of the judge's bench and ran to the rear double doors. A team of police officers stood on the other side and tackled and subdued me. It had been quite evident that I was an escape risk, and by now my feet were shackled as well.

I had told the detectives I had been living in Lowell, and with that information they used my photograph to find out where I had been living and what my true identity was. After that they were able to find out about my pending charges in Indiana and about my police background. This news, combined with my attempted escapes, made it on television and in newspapers. Now it was well known that my identity was John Joseph Piper.

Upon returning me to the jail I was stripped of my clothing, given a slip cover to wear, and placed in a cell on suicide watch. An officer sat in an observation office next to me to watch my every move through a glass window. Lights were on in the room 24 hours a day. There was no bed, only a toilet and a concrete floor. I was held there for a few days, until they determined that I was not suicidal, and moved to maximum security.

Chapter 5

My family was devastated, especially my mother. Friends and former co-workers were shocked. No one could understand what had happened to the person I had been. There was no logical explanation for my behavior. I had lived my life with only one purpose, one dream, and now it was all gone. It was my identity, and without it I did not know who I was, or what I would become. I never allowed anyone into the secret world of my mind. The walls I had built up inside of me were intended to keep everyone out. I never dealt with failure in my life to this degree. My reaction was self-destruction. I had always been the one in control of my life, and my destiny. That all changed now. My future was out of my hands. Now it was going to be determined by the courts and the justice system.

I lost more than my purpose and identity as a person. I lost all dignity and respect I had ever received from anyone. As I sat in a suicide cell before being moved all I could think of was the hope that somehow I would die and escape the pain and humiliation of reality. I wished for death more than anything else. It seemed too difficult to bear all that had taken place, but somehow I managed to survive it minute by minute and hour by hour.

I continued to be held in maximum security and escorted to all court proceedings in leg chains, handcuffs, and a belly chain. This ensured that any future attempts to escape would be futile. The detectives I had previously attempted to escape from showed bitter contempt and anger toward me. My family hired a psychologist to determine if I had mental problems or some kind of breakdown, and when it was determined that there were none I was processed through the system like everyone else.

The days were filled with boredom and a longing for freedom. The only hope I had was wondering when it was all going to be over and I could leave the place I was in. I was confined to the cell 24 hours a day, so it was my only existence at that time. Sometimes I could get my hands on a book to read when a jail volunteer came by with a book cart. Once in awhile ministry volunteers would walk through the block to talk to prisoners about Jesus and the Bible. The prisoner to the left of me, Daryl, often talked to one of the volunteers and he had a Bible they had given him. I had also managed to get a Bible at one point and started talking to Daryl about it. He seemed to be searching for something that would give him answers. I knew what the Bible was about, but I never took the time to try to understand it or follow the teachings. I began reading it while I was in jail, but I was only interested in how it would help me get out.

I remember taking a small Bible with me when I was transported to court for a preliminary hearing on all the charges. I clutched it like it was a life raft. I saw the faces of friends and family who had always loved and supported me. Their faces were confused and bewildered as they looked upon me in my humiliation.

I recalled those brief moments when my mother had tried to tell me about God and how His son Jesus died for me. I remembered the times she had taken me with her to church and I could hardly wait for it to be over. To me it was all just a waste.

The maximum security cellblock I was in had four cells, and my cell was about eight feet wide and ten feet long. There was a steel bunk with mattress pad, bedding, and a toilet with small sink. On one side of me was a man named Daryl who was awaiting trial for murder. On the other side was a man that was half-crazed. Most of the time he talked to himself, and many times he would scream obscenities and scream outbursts in the middle of the night. I ignored communicating with him.

Daryl and I played chess on a board setup outside the bars between our cells and we talked. He talked about Jesus, and I listened. Often we played late into the night when the main lights were off and only a few security lights were left on. The Bible seemed to give him some kind of hope. The charges against him for murder did not look good. Allegedly he was in a drunken rage and he robbed and murdered someone. During the six months I was in the cell next to him he was tried and convicted. The hardest part for him was the daily routine of going and coming back from court. Having to relive the events that brought him to jail through trial was painful. Some nights he would talk after returning, but most of the time he would say nothing. He seemed to take it well when it was over, almost as if it was a relief. Daryl had prayed the sinner's prayer and given his life to Jesus and it gave him hope. When he was sentenced to life in prison without parole he seemed to take it well. He knew he would never live as a free man again, and yet he had a sense of hope that I could not understand. After he was transported to prison I wondered about him, and a part of me felt empty.

The police did not have any evidence against me to link me to other crimes. They wanted to talk to me but my attorney informed them they were not to question me. Since these were my first offenses in Michigan the court was going to be lenient with me. The detectives who had questioned me initially tried to get me to talk but I refused.

A plea bargain was reached and I pleaded guilty to Breaking & Entering, along with Felony Firearms Possession. The Resisting Police and Attempted Escape charges were dropped.

An investigator was assigned to me by the court to conduct a pre-sentence investigation before I was to be sentenced. I knew I would be going to prison, but I had no idea how long it would be. The charges in Indiana against me were not to be held against me, due to the fact that I had not yet been tried or convicted on any of the charges. The investigator recommended that the court sentence me according to Michigan Sentencing Guidelines. The Felony Firearms Possession charge was by law an automatic two-year sentence, to be served before the offense of Breaking and Entering. On August 21, 1987 I appeared before the judge and was sentenced to the two years, and in addition sentenced to one and one half to ten years for Breaking and Entering. As I sat in the back of the sheriff department prisoner van, chained and handcuffed, I saw my father standing out on the street, staring at the van as we pulled away from the court-house. It was the only glimpse I had seen of my father since I was arrested, and I knew I would not see him again for many years.

Within a week I was transferred to Jackson State Prison, also known as the State Prison of Southern Michigan. Built in 1837, it was Michigan's oldest prison, later closing in 2002. At one time it was once the largest walled prison in the world. The main complex was surrounded by a stone wall 14 feet high. The prison housed more than 6,000 prisoners on 56 acres. The huge square cellblocks had five tiers with 600 cells each. Its history was rife with violence.

It was an intimidating sight to see arriving in a prisoner van those many years ago. I was clutched with fear as I went through central processing. It was here that any personal belongings were taken. Prisoners were totally stripped naked, body cavity searches conducted, and inmates showered with soaps and shampoos designed to eliminate lice. It was here that I received my permanent prisoner number, 189648. I no longer had an identity as a person. I was now a number. I was fingerprinted and photographed, given a bedroll, and escorted down a concrete hallway to a large steel door leading to the cellblock. I recall walking through the door, seeing a sight I could only imagine must be similar to hell. The sights, sounds, and smells became etched in my mind like a movie playing over and over again.

(Jackson Prison Yard)

This particular cellblock was known as quarantine, where new prisoners were housed until they were classified and either transferred to another prison, or sent to another cellblock within the main walls to serve their sentence. The processing officer looked at my paperwork and asked me if I wanted to be locked in "Top 6," which was referred to as protective custody, or solitary confinement in an adjoining cellblock. Since I had been a police officer there was a chance I could be recognized and my life endangered. I thought if I could mingle with the population no one would recognize me, and so I was assigned a cell on the main floor where they could keep a closer watch on me.

For the next thirty days I was interviewed and examined by different people, from counselors, doctors, teachers, and psychologists. Within that time they determined my educational status, my needs for counseling and rehabilitation, and based on that they make recommendations. It was later determined that I was not prone to violence, or a physical threat to staff or inmates, and as a result I was classified as a Level 2 prisoner, which is just above minimum security status. My previous attempted escapes from police custody prevented Level 1 status.

Within six weeks of arriving at Jackson I was transferred to a prison in Ionia, only to be transferred again a few weeks later to Muskegon Temporary Facility, a new prison built in 1987. It contained four pole barn buildings which contained living cubicles, occupied by four prisoners each. Each pole barn was separated by residential units of 120 inmates. The entire facility was designed to hold 960 inmates. The grounds had basketball courts, a recreation yard, buildings for education, a prisoner store, mess hall, administration building, and a chapel.

In many ways the grounds were similar to a small college campus, except for the fences with razor wire that surrounded the facility, and the electronic surveillance equipment. The prison perimeter was regularly patrolled by armed guards in vehicles as well. Otherwise it was a nice facility with many conveniences. Each residential unit had a pool table, a TV room, and bathrooms with showers. Prisoners were also allowed to wear personal clothing and have other belongings like small televisions and radios. All personal belongings were marked with prisoner numbers. We were assigned lockers, and could purchase padlocks and footlockers to store our belongings. The prisoner store was open daily for purchasing personal items like toothpaste and soap, but there were other items like snack foods and candy bars.

Other than minor occurrences of theft and occasional fights between inmates this was not a dangerous place most of the time. Order was maintained, daily counts were taken at specific time intervals, and there were many freedoms you would not expect. Looking back on it now it was too comfortable an existence. In many ways it didn't seem like punishment. Every movement was controlled daily, but there were many privileges.

My mother came to visit me weekly. The administration building had a visiting room located in a secure area where I was escorted. Visitors were patted down and allowed to bring in so much money in change for vending machines in the visiting room. Our visits often lasted several hours. I looked forward to our time together, as it was my only contact with the outside world, other than phone calls.

On our visits my mother would also want to pray with me and minister to me. I respected her wishes and followed the old patterns of my life when she had talked to me about God, and as soon as she walked out the door of the prison I had forgotten everything she said. I continued to live in my own world, dreaming about what I could become after my release from prison. I was still a selfish self-serving person.

The routine of prison life for me after leaving Jackson and going to Muskegon Temporary Facility was quiet. I preferred to keep to myself and not get acquainted with anyone if I didn't have to. I spent a lot of time exercising and watching television. I didn't participate in group activities like many of the inmates, and in the evenings after supper I would sit on my bed and watch television or write letters home. I was only interested in seeing the days pass by quickly for me until I could gain freedom.

One of the surprises I received was when my former police academy roommate Mike Rhymer came to see me from South Bend, Indiana. Mike still considered me a friend, even after everything that had happened. He cared about me and still saw something in me that was good. I was grateful for his friendship. Occasionally I would receive a letter from him as well. He came to see me at least twice while I was in Muskegon.

After ten months there I was again transferred to another new prison called Carson City Temporary Facility. I was not happy about the transfer. This place was identical to the Muskegon facility in design, but farther away from my mother. She continued to visit me weekly, making the long drive. Her visits were important to me. Seeing my mother gave me a sense of security. It's difficult to explain, but just knowing she still loved me despite all I had done meant something to me. I was still her son. She also continued to talk to me about God, and tried to get me involved in Bible studies. I humored her, but never got involved in studies with other inmates or went to church services that were held weekly inside the prison facility. I was more interested in myself and my own desires.

About two years had transpired since my original arrest, and I was now eligible to be transferred to a halfway house in Grand Rapids, which was referred to as the corrections center. It was an old motel on Monroe Street that the Michigan Department of Corrections had purchased, and it was used for the rehabilitation of prisoners coming out of prison. Inmates lived there and had the opportunity to get jobs in the community, attend school, and get counseling, or attend meetings for Alcoholics Anonymous (AA), or Narcotics Anonymous (NA).

My initial application for placement at the center was denied because of the charges against me in Indiana. I had never been taken to court, and Indiana had placed a hold on me with the Michigan Department of Corrections upon my release. I contacted my attorney in Indiana and told him to see if he could work out a plea agreement to get the charges against me resolved. I wanted to be free. He contacted the prosecutor in LaPorte County Indiana and worked out a deal. If I would plead guilty to three charges of Official Misconduct all felony charges against me would be dropped. Each charge carried a one year sentence to run consecutively. Good time was to be awarded day for day, to run concurrently with the sentence I had already been serving in Michigan. In plain language my sentence would effectively be "time served." I was manipulating the system, forcing it to work for me, so I could get out of prison.

I had to appear in Indiana to be sentenced. Three Indiana state troopers came to the prison in Carson City to transport me to the jail in Michigan City, Indiana. I knew one of the troopers, Greg Good. I had known him as an officer, and he was an honest and hardworking officer from the Lowell, Indiana District Headquarters. The troopers came in two unmarked cars. I rode in the first car with Trooper Good and another officer. He drove, and I sat handcuffed in the back with the other officer. The third trooper followed behind in another vehicle with a high-powered rifle in the front seat, prepared in case I made any attempt to escape.

I recall my conversation with the officers as we drove to Indiana. They asked me why I had taken the bond money as a state trooper. I still carried anger and bitterness in my heart for the department, and when I answered them I know they were dumbfounded by my response. I told them I never did it, that I was only taking a plea to get out of prison in Michigan. They never asked me any more questions after that.

I was taken to the LaPorte County Jail in Michigan City, where I had made many trips as a State Trooper. I knew all the security of this jail, and everything was familiar to me except the inside of a jail cell, until now. I didn't sleep much that night. I kept reliving my former life as a police officer in my mind. All I could do was look at the ceiling and replay my life as a state trooper over and over in my head. I could see all the triumphs and the tragedies of my life. On this night, and many others, I would have sold my soul if I was able to go back in time to undo the mistakes I had made. I would give anything if I could wake up from this nightmare and be what I once was.

The next morning the three troopers escorted me from the jail to court. I recognized some of the officers from the state police who were there to witness my sentencing. It was uncomfortable being taken to Indiana by the three troopers. They treated me well, but this was the first time I had seen any of my former comrades as a prisoner. It made me feel like a lowly human being. On the outside I covered up what I was feeling and pretended that it was all no big deal, and that it was just a procedure that had to be done. Inside it was tearing me up, and I felt more than humiliated. It was a feeling like having been branded a traitor and going before my accusers to confess my guilt. It would have been more comforting to go before a firing squad. It would have been better to have somehow died in the line of duty with honor. It had finally come to this and I had nothing to say throughout the proceedings. It was the last time in my life that I appeared in an Indiana courtroom.

After the sentencing was completed the troopers escorted me back to Michigan to the prison at Carson City. I can only recall general conversation, in an almost friendly sense. They were doing what they were supposed to do and they did it with dignity. They did not treat me with hostility or a negative demeanor. They followed the *Code of Conduct* that was embedded in their training. They were too kind to me.

Chapter 6

In the weeks to follow I was approved for placement at the corrections center in Grand Rapids, Michigan. It was a halfway house owned by the Department of Corrections (DOC). At one time it was a motel. The state purchased it and converted it into a center for men and women about to be released from prison. It was also operated by the DOC and the same rules applied as they did in prison. It was staffed by prison guards, administrative personnel, and counselors. While there I got a job working for a construction company. It was hard work, but the hours were long, which kept me away from the center and other inmates. Generally I did not care for friendships with inmates. I could never see myself as one of them. I could never fit in. I never trusted Corrections Officers either. Many of them treated prisoners with contempt. I did not want to be near them any more than I had to be.

I was consistent on following the curfew when signing in and out of the facility to go to work each day. On weekends I was able to sign out and spend a few hours with my family. Within thirty days I was placed on electronic tether and sent to live with my mother and my step-father in Grandville, which is a suburb of Grand Rapids. A monitoring device was attached to their phone system, and at different times of the day the system would send a signal and search for the electronic device on my ankle. When not at my job I was supposed to be inside the house. If the device failed to locate me the police would be notified immediately and send an officer to the residence. Failure to be home or at a job was considered escape or attempted escape from custody of the Department of Corrections.

During the time I lived with my parents while on tether and parole they loved me and supported me regardless of what I had done. Many former friends and co-workers had turned their backs on me after I went to prison.

While under supervision I continued to follow all the rules and pay supervision fees that I was required to pay for the privilege of living at home on tether. I was also required to report to a counselor once a week at the corrections center, and occasionally take drug tests. I made very good progress, and after being at home a few months with my mother and step-father I was allowed to get a second job working weekends delivering pizzas. This gave me an opportunity to make more money and spend more time on my own.

My parents were very loving and supportive of me. I went to church with them on Sundays. It was an exercise for me and nothing else. I looked at it more as an opportunity to get out of the house. For my mother it was always more than that. She had been praying for me for years now, hoping that one day God would somehow get my attention and grab hold of me. I was very prideful and my heart was still hardened. I was also very selfish. All I could think about was pursuing new dreams. In my heart I wanted to do good things, but my focus was on myself. I wanted to become someone important, but I was very impatient. I dreamed big dreams, as if I could outdo my former self and become something more significant. I measured my worth by what I did and how much money I could make.

In my private life I never maintained any relationships with women that grew into anything lasting. I still kept connected to Judy in Indiana and her sons through phone calls and letters. Occasionally I went to visit her while on parole and she would come to Michigan. I kept making promises to her about a future together, but all my promises were only words. I was like my father with women because I had relationships with other women as well as Judy, and I was promiscuous.

By May of 1990 I was released from tether and placed on parole. I continued to live with my parents and maintain the two jobs I had. I kept thinking about the future and what I would do with my life.

I started daydreaming about flying airplanes. By summer I had attended a clinic about a career flying airplanes as a professional pilot. I decided to attend ground school to get some training, but after I saw the costs involved for attending a school full-time I knew I could never afford it. I had some money saved, and I began taking lessons from one of the local flight schools at the airport. I enjoyed it so much that I thought seriously that there might be a future for me doing this. Realistically, I had never considered the problems that my criminal history might now cause.

In May of 1991 I was discharged from parole. I felt haunted by the past, not being able to go back to what I had lost, and I hated my name. I still felt contempt in my heart for my father, and I wanted to do away with the name that associated me with him and a family of criminals. I decided to legally change my name, and by the end of summer I had changed my legal name from John Joseph Piper to John Richard Collier. I thought that ridding me of the name Piper would somehow change who I was, but it didn't. Somehow I thought that changing my name would not only separate me from the family history I had been associated with, but it would give me a new start in life, a new identity. I hated what the name had represented.

At the end of the summer I had decided that I would move to Traverse City, Michigan and enroll in their professional pilot program. I had received my private pilot license and thought that if I could get the training and professional certifications with an associate degree I would be able to have a career again. I lived by my dreams, but my dreams always faded away.

I had moved into and rented a small home on the east bay of Traverse City and found two part-time jobs, one driving a taxi cab, and another delivering pizza again. It gave me flexibility to attend college classes. The only problem was that after I had moved and registered I had miscalculated, and there was not enough money or financial aid for me to continue to fly and train. My plans failed again.

While living in Traverse City I talked Judy into moving up from Indiana. She was there less than a month living with me and she felt homesick, so I helped her move back to Evansville. About the time she left was when I knew that my plans for flying would not go through. By then I no longer had purpose again, and my life of crime shifted back into gear.

With no future ahead of me I picked up where I had left off before going to prison a few years earlier. I was alone now in a town I had only known as a young boy growing up, and the circle I followed in my life could not be broken. Drinking and drugging became my way of life again, and I did not even know who I was anymore as a person. I began to target businesses again in three different counties, and followed my previous patterns of safe-breaking(s). I only thought about self, and became filled with greed and anger.

I enticed a friend I had known since my teen years to join me in my life of crime. We had spent much time together as teens and related well because we both came from single-parent families. Rick had always been a friend since I was about 13 years old. We were the best of friends through high school, and we had shared common interests like sports and music. He was also gifted in those areas, and a common bond for us was that neither of us had a father. His parents divorced like mine when he was young, and when our friendship began his mother was raising him, along with a younger brother and two sisters. We became very close and spent most of our days growing up together. My family thought that he had been a bad influence on me and contributed to my life of crime when in fact it was the other way around. I knew Rick well enough to appeal to a part of him that was vulnerable, and he trusted me like a brother, but even more so. His father had been an alcoholic, and died when he was young. I'm sure that in many ways he felt cheated of a real father like I had. The irony of our partnership is that he was married with two small children, and he had a good job. In fact, he worked for the Michigan Department of Corrections. At the beginning I didn't tell him exactly what I was doing, but Rick was no fool and he knew about my past convictions. We spent time together drinking and drugging, and I started bragging to him about easy money, and all he had to do was monitor the police, stay in contact with me by radio, and pick me up when I was finished with the job.

I started to commit many burglaries on my own, and Rick became involved with me later in the fall of 1991. I had been in Traverse City for a couple of months so far, and with winter fast approaching

I wanted to break into as many businesses as possible and take a rest for the winter.

Just after midnight past Sunday on December 16 we drove to the outskirts of the city going west into a rural area. I had targeted a tavern that did a lot of business. We found a small private drive off the county road about a mile from the business and parked there. Rick went with me on foot to watch outside the building in the woods and monitor the police scanner while I entered the building to find the safe. I had pried a rear window and quickly entered the building, making my way to the office where I found the safe. I began to work on the safe and check with Rick occasionally to see if things were quiet. After awhile I failed to notice that my two-way radio had gone dead. I saw lights flashing through the rear of the building and realized that someone was outside.

A deputy sheriff had stopped by to check the building, and Rick was unable to warn me. A wave of fear swept over me as I thought quickly of a way to get out of the building. I found a window to escape from on the west side of the building and exited as fast as I could, taking a wide turn back around the rear of the building. I stopped briefly to see the deputy in the rear parking lot. I was in the wooded area behind him and saw his spotlight focused on the window I had entered earlier.

Rick and I had planned earlier to meet at the car a mile away in case the police unexpectedly showed up. He was supposed to wait for me ten minutes. When I got to where the car had been parked he was gone. He may have panicked, and now I was on my own. All I could see was the outline of the car tracks he had left behind in the snow that was now falling.

It had started snowing earlier, and heavily now. I looked back over my shoulder at the building through the woods almost a mile away and I could see flashlights moving toward me. I knew it was the police. I was out in the middle of nowhere. I really had no bearings, other than the county road that ran east and west. I crossed it from the private drive and began to run across a field, as fast as I could, and as far as I could go. The terrain was not very hilly where I was at the time, and I could see the police lights in the distance, approaching slowly. I could also see police cars on the county road, shining their lights in the fields, trying to find me.

Here I was, running away again, from something, or someone. I could think of nothing else. I ran for a long time, across another road, through woods. I don't know how long it lasted. I lost track of time. I was running like a wounded animal. I could see them getting closer, in front of me, and behind me.

I ran until I dropped of exhaustion. I remember them picking me up out of the snow like a wet mop. Two officers placed me in handcuffs and put me in the back seat of a police car. Then they returned me to the scene of the burglary. There were several other police there, from different agencies. After several officers looked at me to see if they could identify me I was taken to the Grand Traverse County Jail in Traverse City.

At first I refused to talk or give my name. I wouldn't even give them a false name. Even though I refused to talk they kept asking, until finally I told them I was John Piper. I didn't tell them where I lived, but they ran my fingerprints through the Michigan State Police and FBI. Within 24 hours they knew my history, my police background, and my prison record.

The next day a warrant was issued for Rick's arrest. He had been stopped the night before, and he managed to slip through the police dragnet before I was apprehended. He was driving my car, so it wasn't hard for the police to put things together. There was very little evidence against him, only circumstantial. But after the warrant was issued he was taken into custody within forty eight hours.

Things looked pretty bad for me, and I knew it. They had tied me to a burglary and safe breaking, which is a life offense in Michigan. Since I had two prior convictions I was also charged as a habitual criminal, which increases the length of the sentence in Michigan. Later the police tied me to burglaries in Manistee and Leelanau Counties as well, and I faced additional charges of burglary and safe breaking.

I wanted to be dead. I had courted death, running from the police, and I felt hated and despised by them. I had been one of them and had turned, like a traitor in war. I remember one of the court officials telling me what a piece of scum I was, and how I was going to spend the rest of my life in prison. I believed him. I didn't see any way out of this trouble I had gotten myself into. My life, as I saw it, was over.

I refused to contact my family or anyone I knew. I could not spare my mother the pain and anguish she was about to experience again. Somehow I was hoping that my family would never know, but I knew that would not be the case. Within a few days they experienced incredible pain, and especially my dear mother. She had prayed for me all those years, and yet I was lost.

I was truly ashamed of what I had become. I wondered if this person the police had in custody was really an evil man. All of those years I had grown up as a young boy terrified of my father. I just wanted a hero. And when I didn't have one I wanted to become the hero for someone else. But I carried something I could never let go of. It was hatred for my father. It was a deep pain that became anger and rage. It was like a scar I could not get rid of, and it would never heal. No one could ever understand the pain I had felt in my heart. All my life I kept telling myself I would never be like my dad, and now as I sat in a cell with no hope and no future I had become what I hated most. I had become my father.

I never stopped to consider how my actions would affect other people because I only cared about myself and what I could get out of the world. The only things I ever felt were self-gratification and anger. No one was going to tell me what to do or what they thought I should do with my life. It was mine and I was going to do as I pleased no matter what the cost and who it hurt. If I had ever known what real love was I had lost sight of it because I didn't practice it. I was too selfish and full of greed.

Chapter 7

It was about a week before Christmas and I was held in isolation away from the rest of the population for the first week there in the jail. I had not contacted my family and I had no intention of making any phone calls. I was too ashamed of who I was, and wanted so badly to go to sleep and never wake up. I felt completely hopeless, as if I was certainly lost forever.

I had felt the hatred and contempt others had for me after what I had done. Many of the police I had initial contact with treated me with particular distain because of what I had at one time represented. I felt like the lowest kind of human being. I had failed in life and there was nothing I could do to change it.

Something happened after a few days that I was not expecting. A short balding man in his mid-60s stopped at my cell and began to talk to me. He did not stop to curse me or treat me with hatred like I expected. He simply asked how I was and he asked if I wanted to talk. He carried a Bible in his hands. I learned that his name was Bob Hall, and he was the chaplain at the jail. He could see that I was hurting, like a wounded and scared animal. Somehow he seemed to care and he didn't ask for anything from me or start preaching to me. He was a soft spoken man, and gentle. That first time I spoke to him he treated me with kindness, and it made an impression in my mind. We didn't talk about anything in particular. He just wanted to know if I was alright and if there was anything I needed.

The following days were filled with court appearances and meeting attorneys appointed to me by the courts. Due to the pattern of similar crimes that I had committed in neighboring counties I was also charged with burglaries and safe-breaking charges in Manistee and Leelanau counties. I was transported to both counties for arraignment and preliminary hearings, and then later transferred back to the jail in Traverse City where the original charges were filed.

My step-father came to see me at the jail. He drove about 150 miles from Grand Rapids and came alone. He had married my mother when I was in high school, and they had been married over 15 years. My mother was so hurt that she had refused to come and see me. A part of me did not blame her for the way she felt. I had done nothing but think of my own selfish desires, and I never considered the pain I brought upon those who loved me. Even to see my step-father Larry was humiliating for me. I expected judgment from him, but I could see by the pain in his face that he was hurting for my mother more than anything else. After our visit that day I did not know if I would ever see my mother again.

In the days to come I was placed in a jail cell with five or six other inmates. I also saw Chaplain Hall and spent more time talking to him. I felt safe talking about myself with him, and I began to open up about my life. We never talked about my charges, and he never asked me. Something in him brought light into a dark place. I had lost hope for any kind of future, and yet there was something in Chaplain Hall that was full of gentleness and peace. The days continued to pass by and he often got me out of my cell to talk to me on a bench in the hallway between the cells where there was a little more privacy. I looked forward to our talks more and more, and as Chaplain Hall began to share more with me about Christ I listened.

For many years now, even before my arrest, I always placed God in the back of my mind. I had known from going to church with my mother that when people gave their life to Christ they had to surrender to Him, and I always wanted to be the one in control of my life and my destiny. How could I ever trust anyone else with that? But now I was at a crossroad in my life and every road except one lead me to a dead end. I always had to reason everything out, try to figure out the unexplainable, like all of life was a puzzle and every piece fit in somewhere. Thinking I had all the answers led to my downfall. Being full of pride I was never willing to listen to anyone else, or consider another alternative to my way of thinking.

I believe that meeting Chaplain Hall in the Grand Traverse County Jail was a divine appointment for me. Time had run out for me in my life and I felt like more of an outcast in the world than ever before. I had let my family down more than once, and many people who knew me thought that the first time my life turned upside down something snapped in me. Now it must have looked like I was truly a criminal, a thief, and a liar all along.

I had been in the jail for three months and I had to admit to myself that the decisions I made in my life were terribly wrong. I had to take responsibility for the pain and suffering I had brought upon my family and others. Most important, I had to make a decision now that would change the course of my life forever. I had been reading the Bible and attending studies led by Chaplain Hall. I was going to chapel and I was considering my life, and what was left of it. I had never made decisions for my life half-heartedly, and I knew that if I continued to make the decisions in my life that had brought me to this place I would end up in prison the rest of my life, or dead. So in March of 1992, in that jail in Traverse City, Michigan I surrendered my life to Jesus Christ. He became my Lord and my Savior. I was broken now, but it was the only way I could come to Him.

(Chaplain Robert Hall at Grand Traverse County Jail)

That same month my grandfather John, who I had been named after, died unexpectedly in a hospital in Grand Rapids. I had written him a long and painful letter expressing my sorrow for the pain I had caused him and my mother. I learned later that my mother had read the letter to him as he lay in his hospital bed. Unable to speak, he was only able to shed tears, and within a few days he passed away.

My mother had also written me a letter. She had been so hurt by what I had done that she considered that she should disown me as her son. But she was a Christian, and she shared with me that the Holy Spirit had spoken to her heart, telling her that if she rejected me she would be rejecting God. The impact of her letter brought to me the realization that I had almost lost the love of a mother who had done nothing but care for me and love me. I could never count the tears she shed for me or measure the pain that I had brought into her life. So many times when I had been a child and helpless she protected me. Now all she could do was pray for me.

Sometime after I had spent several weeks in jail in Traverse City I was transferred to the Manistee County Jail for a hearing. I was initially taken there a short time after my arraignment in Traverse

City and then returned the same day. This time I was there for a few days, and during that time I was kept in a holding cell apart from the rest of the jail population. Every time I was moved from one jail to another it made me feel uncomfortable. Most of the time I spent in the Grand Traverse County jail, but each time I was moved to Manistee or Leelanau it made me uneasy. The only comfort I knew was that God was with me no matter where I went. I struggled with a fear that I can only try to describe. It was not fear of dying. I think that a part of me had invited death and it didn't take me. The fear I had was living. I had always lived my life according to my own terms, and surrendering it all to God was something foreign to me. Yet even though I was afraid I would cling to God like a child clings to its mother. God became my security and my comfort.

One of the most difficult things for me to do was to forgive myself. I hated what I had become, and it made me question whether all the contemptible things that had been spoken to me were true. When one of the court officers called me scum I believed him. I truly wanted to bury my head in the ground and die. It was only through the kindness of Bob Hall did I realize that I was worth something. He helped me realize how valuable I was to God.

I had such a strong will and determination all of my life, and even though I had made a commitment to give my life over to God it was a struggle for me. It was so hard for me to trust even God. I had to go through a series of inner battles with myself and yield to God. I had to learn to trust him beyond my circumstances. But it didn't come easy. I had to be broken before Him completely through a series of events that were going to take place in my life.

One of those events occurred when I was transferred to the Manistee County Jail for arraignment on burglary and safe breaking charges. I was held in an isolation cell which was a holding tank in front of the officer observation area. There was no peace and quiet. The bright light in the room stayed on 24 hours a day, and there was constant traffic by officers and other inmates. I didn't sleep, and I didn't eat during the time I was there. It seemed like some kind of brainwashing torture to me. My mind was in turmoil over all of the events that had happened and I just wanted it to be over. I could not rest or move. It was as if time were standing still. Something was happening to my spirit during that time because even though I had given my life to Jesus I was a babe in Christ. I was spiritually immature, and in many ways I felt more helpless than ever. I was learning the Word of God, but a battle was raging within me for control. My flesh wanted to take control again, and yet my spirit man longed for God. It was as if He was waiting for me to yield myself to Him, to say, *"Yes, God, I give it all to you."*

After those three days and nights my mother came to see me for the first time since I had been in custody. We sat in a booth, separated by a glass panel. She could see that I had not slept, or eaten, and that I was broken. I shared with her that I had given my life to Christ, and that I no longer lived for myself, but for Him. I didn't have to even tell her or convince her. She could see it on my face. I shared with her the battle that had been raging in my mind for control of my body. But the Holy Spirit had won this battle, and somehow I could feel the presence of God. My mother and I held our hands up to the glass that day in the visiting booth, our palms facing one another. We wept, and prayed.

A couple of days later I was returned to Traverse City after my court hearing and I continued to meet with Chaplain Bob Hall and attend his Bible studies. Repentance was something I began to study and understand. It's not just a desire to change, but making a complete turn away from doing what we know is against God, and choosing to do what is right, what pleases Him. My heart was changing, and I began to know the person Jesus Christ through reading the Word. I had read *Romans 12:2*, which says, *"Do not conform any longer to the pattern of this world, but be transformed by the renewing of your mind. Then you will be able to test and approve what God's will is—his good, pleasing and perfect will."(NIV)* God was doing something to my heart, chiseling away the rough edges, renewing me from the inside out. The new spirit man in me wanted to do the right thing. I wanted to please my Heavenly Father and obey Him. Unfortunately, the sinful nature of my flesh wanted to pull me towards things of the world: greed, lust, the quest for power, selfishness, and dishonesty; in simple terms, sin. The battle for control of my life continued to wage, but it began to change the way I looked at the world, and the way I had looked at myself. God's Word had given me a hope that I did not have before.

Chaplain Hall became a teacher and mentor to me. He not only helped teach me about the life of Jesus, but he showed me what kind of man became a disciple. I took part in every Bible study with him that I could during the week, and I read my Bible daily. Forgotten Man Ministries also supplied Bible studies, and I poured myself into the scriptures to learn the Word of God. In jail most of the time is idle, so it gave me the opportunity to constantly read and study. It wasn't just an exercise for me. It began to give me a new purpose and identity that I never had before. I developed a hunger for God that I had never known, and I wanted to know Him more intimately than ever.

I had been in jail approximately six months and after several court appearances my attorneys had negotiated plea agreements with the prosecutors in the counties I had been charged. In Grand Traverse County the prosecutor offered to drop the charge of Safe Breaking, which could send me to prison for the rest of my life. In exchange I plead guilty to Breaking and Entering and being a Habitual Offender. As part of the deal I also plead guilty to one charge each of Breaking and Entering in Leelanau and Manistee Counties. I agreed and pled guilty to the charges.

My sentencing guidelines in Grand Traverse County called for a minimum of one to three years in prison, and I had been hoping that the judge would follow the guidelines and sentence me accordingly, but it was not the case. I appeared before Judge Rodgers on July 9, 1992. Before I was sentenced he asked if I had anything to say. I had previously remained silent the first time I was ever sentenced for a crime, but not on this day. I expressed my remorse and sorrow for all of my crimes, and for the pain I had brought upon my family. I broke down in court on that day. I had always kept my feelings inside, but on this day I broke down and wept like never before.

When the judge spoke he called me a sophisticated criminal, and said that because of the fact that I had once been a police officer, and educated, that I was to be held to a higher standard. Because I was being sentenced as a habitual offender the minimum sentence he imposed was to be served with no good time, so I was going to spend at least the minimum amount of years behind bars. He sentenced me that day to a term of eight to 15 years. After he had spoken those words my knees just about buckled. I really wasn't expecting that much time, and at the age of 35 it felt like a lifetime to me.

I thought that day was the end of my life. But in the years to come I realized that it was the beginning of my life in Christ. It was the start of God working in me, and it required that time for Him to continue to break the rebellious spirit I had in me to want to do things my own way. I needed that time in prison to change from a man who had always been proud and self-serving to a man who became humble and selfless like Christ, and take on the form of a servant. In time I learned about submitting my life to God completely. The scripture teaches in *James 4:6* that *"God opposes the proud, but gives grace to the humble."(NIV)* I needed His grace to sustain me and take me through the difficult times I faced in prison. Each day I became more thankful for His grace.

Five days after my sentencing in Grand Traverse County I appeared again before Judge Rogers in Leelanau County on the charge of Breaking and Entering. It was more procedural, since the sentence was to be served concurrently, at the same time I was serving the previous sentence I had received. The judge sentenced me to a term of six years and eight months to 15 years. A month later I was also sentenced in Manistee County for a term of five to ten years for Breaking and Entering, also to run concurrently with the other sentences.

I was transferred in July to the prison at Jackson, where I had been sent the first time I went to prison. Other inmates from the county jail that had transferred to prison with me quickly spread the word that I was a former state trooper, and to protect any attempts on my life I was placed in solitary confinement on "Top 6," a cell-block adjoining the main quarantine cellblock. While there I never left my cell without a corrections officer escorting me, even to take a shower.

(Jackson Solitary)

I was there approximately thirty days during my classification process. I never left my cell except for taking tests for re-classification, getting checked out by prison doctors, dentists, teachers, counselors, and psychologists. Meals were brought to my cell, and at 5:00 am each morning I was escorted out to the main prison yard with two other inmates for exercise. One was my co-defendant, and the other was a former deputy sheriff of 15 years who had been sentenced to prison for a sex crime. The bond we shared was that of having served in some capacity in law enforcement. Walking in the yard between the tall cellblocks we could see the 14 foot stone walls, and the gun towers in the distance. It was an odd feeling to know that this was real, to be in the middle of a horrible place one would read about in books or see in movies.

In my cell I had a Bible and paperback books that were passed out by trustees from a book cart. I received letters from my mother and Chaplain Hall in Traverse City. I looked forward to their letters. I had no one else to communicate with, no lifeline to the outside world. I had learned much from the chaplain while in jail, and I developed a hunger for knowing God. Chaplain Bob sent me books written by A.W. Tozier, like *The Pursuit of God*. His letters emphasized the scriptures and gave me self-assurance. My mother's letters always expressed her love, and she shared with me how much God loved me as well.

The prison experience became completely different to me this time. It was not an easy ride. I was about to receive a reality check and see what it was all about and how horrible it truly was. I never saw prison as a place designed to make a person better and prepare them for living in the real world again. What I found out is that prison makes a person bitter, and in rare circumstances better. Most offenders become bitter. The only way I could become better was through Christ. Only He could change me, and God was going to bring people across my path in the following years to touch my life and show me how great His love is.

I had been at Jackson Prison just over a month when I was finally classified as a Level 4 prisoner, which is maximum security. Even though it was determined that I was not a physical threat to persons or property, due to the length of my sentence I was classified at that level. There was a chance that I was going to remain at Jackson and assigned to a cell block there. I was terrified of the possibility. Surviving in the main population for at least eight years would be difficult. I would have preferred to remain in solitary confinement. I did not long for the company of others. I had my Bible and books to keep me occupied. I was beginning to learn how to trust God more.

Chapter 8

I was transported to a new prison in Adrian, Michigan called Gus Harrison Correctional Facility. It was a new state of the art prison that contained cell blocks for different levels of security, from Level 1 to Level 4. Although it was newer in design, in the previous months there had been an escape attempt by maximum security prisoners at Level 4. The prison contained two Level 4 cellblocks. Each was surrounded by razor wire within the main prison complex. Apparently a prison maintenance worker had been working inside the fence near the cellblock and he had a pickup truck. Five or six inmates overpowered him, taking his vehicle and driving it through the fence, then driving through the double-fenced in gates where secure traffic was routed in and out of the facility. A chase ensued with corrections officers in prison vehicles. One inmate was shot and killed by guards and a second inmate was wounded. A short time later the remaining escapees were rounded up and returned to custody.

Needless to say when I arrived at this prison I had heard the story and I sensed a great deal of tension from the guards. They treated inmates with contempt. I was very afraid of this place from the start. Most prisoners in my cellblock were serving life sentences for murder and other heinous crimes like rape, robbery, and attempted murder.

The two-tier cellblock housed 240 inmates, and there were 120 two-man cells with bunk beds. I had been assigned a cell with another man who was a first-time offender serving 12 years for molesting his children. He was not accustomed to prison, and was not institutionalized. We were able to develop a relationship that gave us common ground for mutual consideration and respect.

Most hours of the day we were locked in our cell. We were permitted one hour of free time each day to leave our cells to exercise, watch television or sit outside within the razor wire perimeter of our cellblock. This was done in shifts as a security precaution so that only one of us was permitted out while the other remained in the cell. At meal times the cellblock was released in shifts of sixty men each.

Beyond the gate of the fenced in perimeter of the cellblock was a main yard for exercise. It was about the size of a football field, and had a track for inmates to walk around, a couple of adjoining basketball courts, and a softball field. One hour of each afternoon inmates were given the privilege to go to the yard to walk or exercise. I was thankful for the opportunity to see the sun and breathe fresh air.

At the end of the main yard was a chapel that could hold 75 to 100 people. I soon found out that outside volunteers came in on Sunday mornings to minister to the prisoners. We had to sign up to attend, and were released at a specified time for one hour to attend the service. I took advantage of this opportunity to go to church and fellowship with other men.

Although I was afraid of this prison, there was a high degree of security at all times, and as long as no one knew of my past as a police officer I didn't feel threatened. I maintained a low profile and didn't go out of my way to make friends. But I did begin to seek out other men who were believers. I had seen small groups of men meeting around a picnic table with Bibles, and had later approached one of the men to ask him if I could join them sometime. He welcomed me, and after that I began to join this small group of men each day to read and study the Bible together. I was very quiet then and only asked questions occasionally. I did not like the idea of opening up and talking, especially about myself.

One of the men who led our studies was named Richard Amo. He was in his early sixties and he was serving two back-to-back natural life sentences for drug trafficking in cocaine. Richard was originally from Florida, and had been a huge drug dealer. He had dealt directly with Columbian drug cartels, and was directly responsible for bringing cocaine shipments into south Florida. He also had sold guns to Columbian drug runners, and had federal charges pending against him for that. He was never caught bringing in drugs to Florida, but the federal authorities had been after him for some time. Apparently the feds saw an opportunity to arrest Richard in Michigan when he came up from Florida for a drug deal. It was actually a sting operation with an informant involved and it was specifically designed to bring Richard's operations to an end. It did and he was arrested on federal charges. When he was arrested in possession of cocaine it exceeded the Michigan statutory requirements which allow prosecution and mandatory sentencing for life. As a result the federal authorities turned him over for state prosecution. Once he was convicted for two separate charges he was automatically sentenced to spend the rest of his life in prison.

One of the things that Richard shared with me was that after his arrest he received information regarding the informant that the federal authorities used. His connections with the drug world gave him the power to have the informant killed, and he even considered it. But in the end after Richard surrendered his life to Christ he accepted all responsibility for his crimes and did not want anyone to suffer on his behalf. He wanted to take full responsibility for his actions. Christ had indeed given him a new heart.

Pastor Steve Upshur of New Life Covenant Church had been visiting Richard in the Macomb County jail for several weeks, and from what Richard told me Pastor Steve's persistence paid off. Pastor Steve had a connection with one of Richards's family members and they asked him to go and see Richard in the county jail. Richard told me that even though he had resisted what Pastor Steve shared for some time it eventually paid off and ultimately he surrendered his life to Christ. It was through Pastor Steve that Richard came to give his life to Christ. In the next couple of years I had a chance to meet Pastor Steve in person at Muskegon Correctional Facility when he came with a ministry team to share with the prisoners.

What made matters worse was that Richard had gone so far as to also involve two of his own daughters when he came to Michigan from Florida to make the drug deal and when he was arrested they were arrested as well. As part of his plea agreement with the state later on it was agreed that the charges against his daughters would be dropped. Richard shared with me that they were in fact innocent participants.

I could not fathom spending the rest of my life in this place. To look at Richard you would never be able to recognize he was spending his remaining life here. He was a beacon of light in this dark place. Richard was the first prisoner I had ever seen or met in prison who was so full of the love of Christ that it reflected on his outward man. He was always smiling, full of joy, and had a peace about him that only God can give.

As I continued to attend the studies with the small group of men I developed a friendship with Richard. He had been incarcerated a little over four years when we met.

We would often walk the prison yard in the afternoons for the one hour we received, and we would talk about the Lord. I was still a very immature, young Christian, and I was drawn to Richard because I saw Christ in him. Early in our friendship I had asked him to share with me how he had given his life to Christ, and he told me his story about coming to Christ while in the county jail, somewhat similar to my story. As I stated earlier Richard resisted receiving Christ at first. Making such a commitment was difficult for him, and he did not want to make it unless he was going to do it with all his heart. God got through to Richard, broke down all barriers, and he stepped out in faith to receive Jesus Christ. Looking at Richard I could see what the Bible describes in *Philippians Chapter 4, (4-7) "Rejoice in the Lord always. I will say it again: Rejoice! Let your gentleness be evident to all. The Lord is near. Do not be anxious about anything, but in everything, by prayer and petition, with thanksgiving, present your requests to God. And the peace of God, which transcends all understanding, will guard your hearts and your minds in Christ Jesus."* In this place where we were the natural man could look at Richard and never recognize the peace that shone through him, unless that man knew Christ.

I began to look at Richard as a spiritual father to me, and I poured my heart out to him one day as we walked in the prison yard.

I told him everything about my background as a police officer, my triumphs, and the tragedies of my life that had led me to prison. I believe that he saw something in me that I had not been able to show anyone. It was my heart. Once shattered and broken, I felt the pieces of my heart mending because God had used Richard to touch my life.

It was not only my life that he touched. Others in the prison recognized something in Richard as well, even officers. If you asked Richard how he was on any day he would respond, "If I was any better I couldn't stand it." It was a standard response for him when anyone greeted him and asked how he was. It was easy to tell that he really meant it. There were times that I saw Richard in the office of the shift sergeant, and other occasions where guards went into his cell because they had asked Richard to pray for them. As I recall those days I recognize that it was by the power of God and by the presence of Christ living in Richard that these things could happen.

It gave my mother great peace when I shared with her about Richard Amo. She could recognize how God was using him to teach me many things, and as God used him in my life it gave me more peace than I had ever received since I was in prison. The fear that Satan had been using against me was weakening, and it was through Richard that I developed a closer walk with Christ. I began to realize more each day that the years I was spending in prison were nothing in comparison to what Richard was facing. I desired more than anything to get to that place in my life where I would have the same peace he had.

I had been in maximum security about six months when I was reclassified to go to Level 2. This meant that I would be transferred to a different cell block in the prison with more privileges and more freedom. The counselor in my cell block found it hard to believe when I told him that I didn't want to transfer, and that I wanted to stay. It made no sense to him. I couldn't tell him that the real reason I wanted to stay was because of Richard. I did not want to leave him. I had become attached to him, and going to a lower level in security meant that I would never see him. More likely than that, I would probably never see him again, and it would be very hard for me to detach myself from him. But I had no choice in the matter, and within a few days a guard gave me a duffle bag to pack my belongings for the move.

Richard and I talked before I moved from the cell block. He was happy for me because moving on to lower security was a good thing for me. We promised to write letters to each other, which was allowed. As I gave him a hug and told him I loved him he smiled at me, told me he loved me too, and he watched me walk out the gate down the walkway that led to the other part of the prison. In the weeks and months to come we promised we would write each other, sharing how Christ had been working in our lives, and what, if anything else, was new.

After I was moved to another part of the prison at Adrian to medium security I stayed connected to Richard through the letters we shared. Most of what we talked about was Christ working in us and those around us who were brothers in the Lord. I missed walking the yard with Richard as we had done on a daily basis, but the solitude that I began to feel during this time was a growing time for me. It brought me into a closer relationship with Christ. He was my constant companion from early morning until bedtime.

Prayer became a way of life for me. I prayed before morning devotions, before my studies, while jogging in the prison yard, and everywhere I went. *1 Thessalonians 5:17* says we are to *"Pray without ceasing."* It became ingrained in me to pray constantly, and it gave me a peace that surrounded me with God's presence.

I can remember walking in the prison yard and after a rain shower seeing a rainbow peeking through the sky, reminding me of what God said in His Word.

And God said: "This is the sign of the covenant which I make between Me and you, and every living creature that is with you, for perpetual generations: I set My rainbow in the cloud, and it shall be for the sign of the covenant between Me and the earth. It shall be, when I bring a cloud over the earth, that the rainbow shall be seen in the cloud; and I will remember My covenant which is between Me and you and every living creature of all flesh; the waters shall never again become a flood to destroy all flesh. The rainbow shall be in the cloud, and I will look on it to remember the ever-lasting covenant between God and every living creature of all flesh that is on the earth." And God said to Noah, "This is the sign of the covenant which I have established between Me and all flesh that is on the earth." (Genesis Chapter 9)

It was in these brief moments that I could smile inside and say, "Thank you Lord for loving me, and for giving me a peace I never had before." God constantly reminded me that He would never change and He always kept His Word.

I continued my correspondence with Chaplain Bob and my mother. I continued to attend the church services at the chapel when permitted, and I began study courses through the Salvation Army. I had been taking study courses through Forgotten Man Ministries since I had been in the county jail, and I continued these studies as well. For the next 12 months I did not form any close relationships, but focused on my Bible studies, my letters, and my visits with my mother, Chaplain Bob and his wife Jamie, and sometimes my sister or a family friend. I also made phone calls to them as well on a regular basis, which was a blessing for me.

My life became one of regular solitude. Early mornings I read my Bible, studied, and when the yard opened I would go out to the track to run five miles, praying during that time. I would listen to tapes by pastors in different ministries that I received from Chaplain Bob. I would often look toward my old cell block for Richard, but never see him. Although I felt an inner peace from knowing that my Lord Jesus was with me each day there was a loneliness I can only describe as a sort of melancholy feeling. I didn't have any close brothers in Christ, or friends to speak of. It was as if I existed within myself apart from the rest of the world around me.

Chapter 9

I had been at the Gus Harrison Regional Facility for 18 months. Now a new chapter began in my spiritual journey. In the early spring of 1994 I was transferred to Muskegon Correctional Facility. It was one of the few prisons in Michigan that offered adult education and training programs in horticulture, auto mechanics, and culinary arts. Another one of the advantages of this place was that many programs were carried out with the help of a variety of Muskegon community groups. Volunteers, made up primarily of local clergy and lay people, assisted the prison chaplain in providing religious instruction. MCF, as it was referred to, was at that time a Level 3 prison. I had requested the transfer to be close to my mother, and this was a mixed facility, with Level 2 prisoners as well. Many of the prisoners were serving life offenses for murder and other serious crimes, but this was a facility that rewarded prisoners for good behavior with many privileges not found at most state prisons. For that reason most inmates preferred to stay out of trouble and on good behavior. There were, however, exceptions.

When I arrived at the prison with a small group of other prisoners we were told that just a few days before an inmate had been murdered in the prison yard. Apparently he had been stabbed over a drug deal and bled to death before getting medical help. I felt uneasy as I entered this place surrounded by three fences with razor-ribbon wire, gun towers, armed patrols, cameras and electronic detection systems. From the outside it looked intimidating with all the security, but inside the facility the prison grounds were well groomed, with lots of trees, and prison cellblocks (housing units) that resembled college dormitories. Walkways connected the main yard between the housing units, and there were basketball courts and horseshoe pits. The main school facility had a gymnasium, classrooms, an auditorium that also doubled as a theatre, and the prison chaplain's office. There was also a small quartermaster building for prisoners to receive personal property after they were properly processed into the facility. Beyond the yard was a gate leading to the main recreation yard, which was huge. Surrounded by the razor wire and gun towers were two well-maintained softball fields, a hard surface track, and a recreation office for prisoners to check out bicycles and athletic equipment.

There were many programs to take advantage of, especially for religious groups. The Department Of Corrections made accommodations for all religious groups, including Jewish, Christian, Muslim, and others. I was especially thankful that I was able to come to a place where I would have the privilege to have access to more programs and Christian services. Any inmate that had ever been to this prison would undoubtedly agree that it was by far the best prison in the state.

The visitor facility was the nicest I had ever seen, with an outdoor visiting area with picnic tables and umbrellas, trees for shade, and a small walkway around the visitor area for people to stroll around. When people came to visit me we could take a Bible into the main visiting area inside, or go outside during nice weather to read and share the Word of God. My mother would come every week to see me and fellowship. Chaplain Bob Hall and his wife Jamie would also come from Traverse City when they were able. I was fortunate to receive visits from other family like my sister and her daughter on occasion. I was thankful for each opportunity to spend with someone.

Writing letters was almost a daily occurrence for me. I continued my correspondence with my friend Richard Amo back in Adrian. It was a way for us to share about what God was doing in our lives. I never stopped writing to Richard as long as I was in prison, and continued to communicate with him in the years to come. I also continued to write to Chaplain Bob. He and his wife Jamie continued to send me books through the Forgotten Man Ministry to feed my growing hunger to know God. They constantly encouraged me and loved me as a son through every phone call, letter, and visit.

I settled into MCF assigned to Aspen Unit. All of the housing units were named after trees, like Aspen, Birch, Cedar, and so on. At that time Aspen Unit was for all new prisoners. It also had a separate wing for isolated prisoners known as segregation, or as prisoners called it, *"the hole."* In the housing unit new prisoners would go through a process of orientation to determine if they were required by their classification to attend school, work at a prison job, attend Alcoholics Anonymous (AA), and receive some kind of specialized training.

The cells in the housing unit did not have bars (except for segregation), but steel doors with thick, unbreakable glass windows. Each room housed two inmates, each with a key to the room. My roommate Joe was a first-time offender and a bit younger than I was. Joe was a former school teacher serving a lengthy sentence for a sex offense. Over time we developed a friendship, and we got along so well that we hoped we would be able to continue rooming together as long as we were at this facility. We developed trust between us and prison is definitely one place where a person needs to know that their belongings won't disappear mysteriously. A trustworthy person sharing the same living space was very important. During our orientation we were both able to get jobs working in Aspen Unit, and because of that we were able to stay there after our orientation was completed. Our friendship also grew because we were both Christians. I learned that Joe had given his life to Christ, and I came to trust him completely and eventually shared with him my background as a police officer. Our friendship developed to where I saw Joe as a brother, and we not only shared a commitment to live for Christ, but we exercised together and spent many days talking about God.

Over time I learned about the many programs and services provided by the prison chaplain. He was a man that I recognized as one who truly cared about the salvation of inmates. He did not look at us just as prisoners, but as men who needed salvation. Many live without hope, and Christ is the only way for men and women in prisons to find it.

What I began to recognize is that all of my life I had lived for an identity that I had given myself. When it was taken from me I had nothing left, no plan, no purpose, and no identity. I didn't know who I was anymore or where my life was going. I was without hope, and I was lost. But as Christ continued to live and grow inside of me my identity became clear. It didn't matter anymore what I would do the rest of my life. Whether I worked in a factory, in construction, at an office, or whatever, my whole purpose for living was Christ. He gave me hope. He became my reason to live.

Almost every night of the week volunteers from neighboring communities came into the prison. On Sundays visiting ministers and pastors came to lead our services in the auditorium. We also had services on Sunday and Wednesday evenings. On weeknights volunteers would come in to hold Bible studies. All of these people came from different churches and denominations. The common bond was Christ.

I know I was blessed to be in this place where God was using many different people to sow seeds into my life that would help me grow and mature spiritually. I can name a couple of people, in particular, that God used, because later in my life God brought us back together again. One of those people was a Grand Rapids police officer who came into the prison once a month on Sunday mornings. As a volunteer, Charlie Myers considered only that he loved the Lord, and God had given him a heart to serve, to come into a prison and minister to criminals. But Charlie did not see us as criminals. He saw us as men who were hungry for God. He never considered himself better because of his position, but he reached out with the love of Christ to make a difference, to touch our lives. He was a big man, about 6'4" or 6'5" in height, intimidating in stature, but his countenance was gentle and kind. All those times he came into the prison I had never talked to him or met him personally, but as I sat in the auditorium and received the Word of God that he shared I never forgot him. I know that Charlie recognized a hunger to know God in this place because of the passion the men showed, especially during the praise and worship. Different inmates used the gifts they possessed to lead the rest of us, and many were very good musicians and singers.

There was also a dear lady that Charlie brought with him every once in awhile. Judy Buffum was a striking lady with a beautiful countenance. What I remembered about her most was her incredible voice. She sang with the voice of an angel. This lady glowed with the light of Christ in her, and there was a powerful presence about her. One could only sense that the Holy Spirit surrounded her. I was so thankful to see that she was not afraid to come into this place of murderers, robbers, thieves, and others to share the love of Christ. I had no idea those many years ago, that as God used her to also sow seeds into my life He would use her again to touch my life in the years to come.

As God used people like Chaplain Bob Hall to mentor and teach me about Christ, He also used relationships that I developed with some of my Christian brothers to shape the person I was becoming. In jail, I had seen what has been commonly referred to as *"jailhouse preachers,"* people who appear to be religious while in jail, then go back to living as they had previously lived, with no actual change or sign of repentance. What I found was that most all men who have nothing to gain by it, especially those who are serving life sentences, are the real thing. One of the things God gave me was the ability to discern between truth and a lie. It wasn't because of the fact that I was once a police officer. I had developed what is sometimes called a sixth sense, but it was a gift from God. My nature had always been to suspect everyone I came into contact with. My father had always made promises to me as a young boy growing up, and he had never kept them. So it was only natural for me to never believe anything or anyone without proof. When God showed me through his Word in *Hebrews Chapter 11* that faith *"believes without seeing,"* I understood that true faith is based on a spiritual relationship with God. And that word *relationship* became the key for me. I wasn't just getting religion in jail and prison. I was developing a relationship with the Creator of the Universe, the God of all creation. In prison you live very close to everyone, and it doesn't take long to see if the outside of a man is the same on the inside. It's like the glass house. Even though you live inside, everyone can see through you. My Christian brothers were men I came to trust and love. Like Richard Amo, I was given a family of believers to share my faith and my hope with. These were not men that I looked at on the outside because of their crimes. In *1 Samuel Chapter 16* it says that God looks at the heart. And that is the same way I saw my brothers in Christ.

During my stay at MCF I also had the opportunity to meet Pastor Steve Upshur who had led Richard Amo to the Lord years before. Pastor Steve came to MCF on more than one occasion with a team of men to minister to the inmates. I was happy to see him and make the connection of knowing our mutual friend and brother in Christ. Pastor Steve continued to see Richard and have contact with him so it was a great joy for me to find out more about how Richard was doing and to share with Pastor Steve how Richard had been such a great friend and spiritual father to me during my time at the prison in Adrian.

MCF was the first prison that I became more involved with other men other than through church services and Bible study. Before coming there I had always isolated myself from becoming involved in intramural activities. I had always loved team sports, but in prison I had avoided them until MCF.

One of the men I got to know in Aspen Unit was a man named Sam. He was about five to ten years older than me, and he was a Warden's forum representative for inmates. He was trusted by the staff and inmates. During my initial orientation in Aspen Unit, Sam and another inmate conducted the orientation. After I got a job as a porter in the unit doing janitorial work he approached me one day to ask me if I played softball. I had played some baseball in high school and college so I said yes. Sam was coaching the unit softball team and he wanted me to try out. I had always loved sports, and even though I had previously chosen not to get involved I decided to give it a try. After tryouts I ended up playing second base.

I had never realized before getting involved in prison athletics that there is a great deal of competition, and that there are several gifted athletes in prison. When I got involved playing softball it was organized. There was a league with one or two teams from each housing unit, and a regular schedule of games was setup. Practices were setup by coaches to use the softball fields, and inmates umpired the games. The umpires were men who had taken some training, and they worked under a civilian employee in the recreation department who was their supervisor. These men wore umpire hats and shirts and were very serious about their job during the games.

The level of competition was tremendous, and crowds of prisoners would gather on the sidelines to watch and cheer the teams from their housing units. Sometimes games got heated, but the umpires always maintained control of the game, and I never saw a fight. I grew to enjoy this part of prison life and looked forward to it. Not only did I get good exercise, but I had always been a serious competitor and this gave me a chance to excel in something.

It was also good to see men who were outcasts from society learning to do something as a team. We had to rely on each other and play as a single entity. Sam was a very good coach. He was disciplined, and he used it to shape us into something better than we thought we could be. He expected us to show up and practice, take direction, and taught us basic principles of the game. Men who failed to practice, weren't disciplined, and didn't show dedication to the game did not last. As a result of Sam's coaching and our efforts our team won the first league championship that spring.

I also got to develop some very good relationships with men that I would not have known, had I chosen not to play softball. Sam was probably the first because he was my coach and I worked as a porter in the same housing unit. We became friends, and Sam knew I was a Christian. I had shared with him many times how Christ had taken the broken person I was and made me into something new. Many times we talked, and eventually I got Sam to do Bible studies with me. Often times I would sit in the prison yard under a tree with him and we talked about the Lord. I noticed after a time that he read his Bible more and more. God was using me to reach out to him.

One of the men who umpired became a friend off the field. His name was David. He was also a believer in Christ. He had been in prison almost 20 years. Our friendship began out of mutual respect for the game, and his authority on the ball field was well known and respected. After we became friends we developed a close relationship and trust based on Christ. David was also a competitor, and later in the summer he took a break from umpiring to play softball with me on a team coached by Sam. We won another champion-ship as a result, and during that time I got a closer look at the man inside David. He was about five years older than me and was gifted with gardening and crafts. Even after I left MCF we corresponded through letters and I prayed that one day he would be granted a parole. That prayer was answered when God blessed David with freedom seven or eight years later.

I also became very actively engaged in weight lifting while at MCF. I had started weight training at Adrian while in Level 2, and after I arrived at Muskegon I started again. My roommate Joe had expressed a desire to get involved, and when we started the two of us would go to the weight pit early each morning. It was located inside a separate fenced in area just inside the main prison gate with a gun tower overlooking. Anywhere from 50 to 75 men at a time might be lifting weights. It was a scene reminiscent of movies you have probably seen, muscular men with tattoos and bandanas, sweaty and hot pounding heavy weights on benches. Occasionally there were confrontations over using a bench or weights that resulted in a fight or a stabbing, but they were rare occurrences with the gun tower nearby. However, intimidation sometimes played a factor.

Joe and I avoided confrontation. After we had developed some relationships with men who were Christians our group grew to three or four. The presence of more individuals helped as a deterrent to individuals that would try to intimidate us.

Even though I was in prison I had come out of my shell at MCF. I was able to let some walls down to experience some relationships and friendships with men that I would otherwise have never known. To this day I am thankful that God brought those different men into my life.

(Michigan Prison Visit – Chaplain Bob & Jamie with John)

I never took for granted the privileges I had in prison, and I was sometimes reminded of where I was when sirens would sound and emergency count went into effect. These routinely took place at unexpected times, but there were incidents in the prison, like assaults, and attacks on staff that sent the prison into a state of lock-down for hours. One of those incidents involved inmates that had taken a female guard hostage in a housing unit behind the one I resided in. By watching from my cell window during the ordeal, I witnessed prison guards in riot gear, the Michigan State Police Tactical Team entering the cell block, and an ambulance taking away injured staff.

I believe that God kept His hand of protection upon me in this place during these difficult times. I recall other times when I had passed by places within the prison just moments before or after a stabbing or attack took place. It was as if God had placed a hedge of protection around me to shield me from these things. Because of violence and assaults, over the course of time, prison officials began to take away many privileges all inmates had benefited from at MCF. Nonetheless, as I witnessed these things happening I remained thankful to God for each blessing He gave me, and for his protection.

During the approximately two and one half years I remained at MCF God had taught me so much. I had studied the Bible, read it cover to cover more than once, and saw the scriptures come to life for me. The first scripture I memorized and have always kept close to my heart was that shared with me by my mother. Many times when I felt troubled and helpless she encouraged me with these words, *"Trust in the LORD with all your heart and lean not on your own understanding; in all your ways acknowledge him, and he will make your paths straight."(Proverbs 3:5, 6 NIV)* Those words would give me comfort when I couldn't understand why things happened the way they did. Sometimes during those years of imprisonment my natural man wanted to try to figure things out again and question why. I had to learn to trust God, and rely on Him for all things.

I remember distinctly the first time I had read and understood *2 Corinthians 5:17*, which says, *"Therefore, if anyone is in Christ, he is a new creation; the old has gone, the new has come!"* I realized that even though I was in prison, the person I had been no longer existed. It was as if that person had died, and was born anew. God gave me comfort knowing that my future no longer had to be determined by my past. The Lord not only forgave my sins, but he forgot them, and gave me a new life.

One of the blessings I received in prison was baptism. When I was born I was baptized into the Catholic faith, but never in my life had I actually been fully immersed and baptized until the opportunity came along while I was in MCF. The chaplain had arranged and provided for a square tank to be filled with water one Saturday morning during the summer. A group of about a dozen men gathered outside behind the main school building around the tank to pray, and one by one we climbed up and into the tank, each stating our declaration of faith in Jesus Christ as Lord and Savior. A pastor prayed and submersed each one of us. I recall the peace and joy I felt that morning, knowing that I had taken an obedient step in pursuit of the new life I had received from God.

I had come to a new level of maturity in my walk with Christ. I had to learn to trust God in everything, including those things I had no control over. One day my mother and my sister came to visit me unexpectedly. During the entire time I was in prison I also communicated with Judy back in Indiana. I still cared a great deal about her and we talked through letters and occasional phone calls. There were times that I did not speak to her or hear from her for awhile but it was normal. Our lives were separated by several hundred miles. On this particular day when my mother and sister came to visit I learned from them that Judy recently had undergone emergency brain surgery for a tumor. It was later determined that the tumor was in fact cancer. Even though she had survived the surgery her doctors had told her that she would not survive more than a few months because the cancer was terminal. My initial response was that I felt devastated. After our visit I returned to my cell block dazed and confused. But after the initial shock wore off I remembered that God's word says, *"For I know the plans I have for you," declares the LORD, "plans to prosper you and not to harm you, plans to give you hope and a future." (Jeremiah 29:11)*. I was not going to stand by and just wait for Judy to die. I began praying for Judy and writing regularly and calling to encourage her with those words and the love of Christ. I began to speak blessing into her life. There had been times in the past when I had talked to Judy about my faith in Christ, but she had a difficult time believing that I had changed. Through the next several months God continued to use me to minister to her, and during that time she told me she had given her life to Christ and that she was learning to trust God with her circumstances. Something was happening inside her and the few months that she had been given to live turned into several more. She became more determined than ever that she was going to live.

Chapter 10

In the fall of 1996 I was unexpectedly transferred to another facility in Muskegon. Before my transfer from MCF the climate was changing. The Department of Corrections had been making changes to the facility to tighten security. The landscaping of the main yard with all the trees was slowly being eliminated as they began to cut down trees, and freedom within the main yard was being restricted. Open yard was no longer allowed, except on the main recreation yard beyond the main yard. Only inmates with legitimate passes were allowed to travel on the grounds of the main yard. The higher security prisoners that were being transferred into MCF were part of the reason.

There had also allegedly been a sexual assault in the visitation area of the prison. Additional restrictions were put in place to heighten security. As a result, many of the privileges inmates had previously enjoyed were lost. Lower security inmates were being moved to make room for higher security inmates that were being moved into MCF. It was never easy being transferred. It was always unexpected, and I never knew where I would end up. It was even more difficult to say goodbye to brothers I had come to know and love in Christ. There were a couple of men that I stayed in touch with like Sam and Dave, and my roommate Joe. These men had become like family to me, and it was encouraging to be able to write letters, share burdens, and give praise through writing. As always I continued my correspondence with Richard Amo too and informed him of the changes that had taken place.

For a short six months I was sent to Muskegon Temporary Facility, which was located close to MCF. Going there was a bit eerie for me, as it was the pole barn facility I had gone to nine years earlier when I went to prison for the first time. The physical location and layout of the facility did not change, but there were some good programs.

The biggest change at this facility was that the Department of Corrections was transforming it into a treatment facility for sex offenders. My stay here was going to be short. But after I arrived I found many different programs available and I was going to take every opportunity to participate in any program that was going to help me meet every requirement that the Department of Corrections had placed upon me.

It was here that I was able to work with computers for the first time in the prison school. There was a vocational program, and I wanted to learn something new and take advantage of any training I could get. It was challenging for me, but I found that each day I went to school and applied myself I began to grasp and get a feeling for computers. I discovered that it was something I grasped quickly and I enjoyed the challenges.

I also took advantage of attending counseling classes for drug addiction and alcoholism. I had never seen myself as a drug addict or an alcoholic, but I remembered the self-destructive lifestyle I had adopted toward the end of my police career. There was a history in my family of drug and alcohol addiction on my father's side, and prison counselors had recommended these classes for me during my classification when I was at Jackson Prison.

Some inmates resented having to attend these classes, since it was a requirement when being considered for parole or release. I prayed and asked God to reveal to me those things that I needed to understand and my mind and heart was opened. I learned much from what these classes taught me, and I began to recognize the patterns of addiction in my family history. After a time I looked forward to these classes, and my schooling. God was using this time to teach me things that I had not considered.

While at this facility I also had been blessed with a chaplain that provided programs and services that would help me continue to be fed spiritually by volunteers. I was among the first group of men in a Michigan prison that participated in an event held inside the prison by Promise Keepers. I had never attended such an event before. Our small chapel was packed with volunteers and inmates, praising and worshipping God, and embracing the *Seven Promises* of the organization.

Although my stay at this facility was going to be short, I also had an opportunity to connect with a former deputy sheriff I had walked with in the prison yard at Jackson who was serving a 15-year prison sentence. It had been over four years since I had talked to him, and I found that Brian had also given his life to Christ some years earlier. There were over 40,000 inmates in Michigan prisons at that time, and yet we had the chance to meet again as brothers in the Lord. I spent many mornings walking with Brian in the prison yard at Muskegon Temporary Facility now, much like I had done a few years earlier with Richard Amo. Brian was a broken man. He still carried much pain, but not for himself. It was for his children. He loved them dearly, and had not seen them for years since going to prison. His heart ached for them, and for the pain he had brought into their lives. I found out years later that Brian died in prison. My prayer was that before that happened he was able to see his children one last time. For whatever pain he caused to suffer on others and himself he received forgiveness from God, and now he is no longer lost. He's with the Savior.

When I was again transferred on the first day of spring the following year I was not surprised. My security classification had been lowered to Level 1 (trustee), and I was sent north with several other prisoners. The Upper Peninsula of Michigan has several prison camps spread out in the vast wilderness. Along the way I stopped at two camps before ending up at Marquette Branch Prison located on the shores of Lake Superior. Although the southern half of Michigan was experiencing spring weather the Upper Peninsula was in the midst of a snowstorm, receiving 23 inches of snow on the day I arrived at the prison. I was not happy, particularly because I was now over 400 miles from my mother, and I expected to rarely receive any visits. What I did not consider was that God was going to use my stay here to prepare me for the journey home.

The main prison was built in 1889 and very similar to Jackson Prison in Southern Michigan. The 14 foot brick walls with the gun towers made it look very similar in appearance. I was thankful to be sent to the trustee housing units outside the walls. For the three days I spent there I was examined and classified to be sent to the prison farm six miles south of the main prison.

The Mangum Farm housed approximately 65 inmates in two military-style barracks. A ten foot chain link fence surrounded the facility, which stood atop a bluff overlooking Lake Superior, thousands of acres of wilderness, and fields for harvesting hay and corn during the summer. Inside the facility there was a weight room, a small library, a recreation room with a pool table and television, a laundry room, and a mess hall. Outside the building inside the fenced perimeter were a basketball court and a huge recreation yard about two to three acres in size. A small path for walking or jogging was used by inmates for exercise. Two corrections officers provided supervision for the trustees at all times, and during the day two civilian supervisors took trustees outside the fence to work on the farm.

The Mangum Farm was a cattle farm, with approximately 150 head of beef. The cattle were raised and slaughtered as food for the prison population, while the trustee division at the main prison had a dairy farm where cows provided milk for the prisoners. I felt very isolated out here after becoming accustomed to larger prison populations, but in many ways I became thankful for the great beauty and peace that now surrounded me.

After my classification I was assigned to work outside the fence on the farm with cattle. I had never done anything like this in my life, and I was a bit squeamish at first, especially being around bulls that weighed over 1,000 pounds. But as I learned about handling cattle, feeding them, caring for them, and doing other chores, my dread became something I looked forward to.

The work was very hard, especially during the summer months when we worked 12 hour days, bailing hay, filling the barns. The prison also leased land from adjoining farms, and we would travel to these farms to also work, walking the fields in the spring to pick up stones from the fields, then planting, and harvesting.

The first full winter I was there in Marquette we received over 26 feet of snow. Sometimes it was dreadful trying to move cattle under those conditions. They were kept in five separate pens, starting with the calves, and so on. During the coldest weather we would herd the cattle into the barns and would have to force them out to clean the manure using tractors and shovels. On days like those the smell would go right through the clothing we wore. We got used to it, but the other trustees in the main barracks complained as soon as we came in. As soon as we entered the building we stopped at the main laundry to strip off our work clothes and head to the showers. I grew accustomed to the hard work, and it became second nature to me.

It was difficult to be so far away from my mother, but I telephoned her each week and wrote letters. I continued my correspondence with Chaplain Bob, and called his home weekly as well, talking to him and his wife Jamie. I spent many evenings in the library to write. I enjoyed the peace with other trustees, and took every advantage to stay in contact with family and friends. My letters to Richard and some other brothers in prison also continued.

A big adjustment for me was that I didn't receive visits very often, and I valued them even more. Every few months my mother would take the long drive, and stay for a couple of days to see me. Visits took place at the main prison, so a guard would drive a van to pick me up at the farm and return me afterwards. Bob and Jamie Hall also came to minister to me and have fellowship. They had been faithful to come and visit me since I entered the jail in Traverse City years before. It was no different here. As they had previously traveled to the different prisons I had been in before they also traveled to Marquette to visit me for 2-3 days at a time. They would stay at a local motel and I welcomed our time together. They had become more than mentors to me. They were dear family and I grew to love them a great deal.

I was also able to begin a relationship with family that I had never really known as a young boy growing up. My mother had an older sister named Rose who lived in the Upper Peninsula with her husband Jim. Uncle Jim had established a mission in Manistique called Good Neighbor. They reached out to the poor and helpless in their community to help people in need of food, clothing, and shelter. Although their ministry did not provide shelter, they worked with businesses and community leaders to help people find a place they could afford to live.

They lived in the town of Manistique, Michigan, about 90 miles south from the main prison, which is located on the northern shores of Lake Michigan, bordering the south side of the Upper Peninsula. They were Christians, but did not know me personally, and were reluctant to come and see me. They had known of me and heard of my criminal exploits, but had never known me personally. After their initial visit their reluctance faded and we developed a relationship that grew. My Uncle Jim and Aunt Rose became very precious people to me, full of the love of Christ. They were people who had little, but gave all they could. I considered my visits with my aunt and uncle as precious. We came to know each other in a prison visiting room, and the common bond we had was Jesus. They were not just an extension of my mother, but of God, reaching out to me in a faraway place. For as long as I was in Marquette they continued to come and see me at least once a month, and in warmer weather, more often. I loved them dearly.

I grew to appreciate many things about the prison farm. It was not like normal prison life with thefts, assaults, fighting, and strife between inmates. Outside of the barracks I could see such beauty for miles. It was nothing in comparison to the steel and concrete I had been accustomed to with razor wire fences, gun towers, and armed patrols. The officers treated the inmates well too. It was comforting in many ways to be at such a place.

I received freedoms I had not been used to. Working outside the gate of the main barracks on the farm I was often left to work alone with other inmates to manage the cattle, take care of feeding, cleaning barns, and doing other chores. The two civilian workers that ran the farm were decent hard working men from the Marquette area, and as a regular part of our jobs we often accompanied them in vehicles into the city of Marquette to pick up paper from businesses for recycling. Sometimes we traveled to the dairy farm at the trustee division of the main prison to pick up milk or equipment for the Mangum Farm.

In the months of the first summer the inmates worked in teams to pick up hay in the fields. Although it was hard work there was something about it that felt rewarding, as if we were somehow making a difference. Many times I had the opportunity to drive a prison flatbed truck with some of the other trustees on board as we went through the fields. I considered it a privilege to drive a vehicle again, especially under these circumstances.

I had missed the spiritual relationships with inmates that I had at other prisons like Adrian and Muskegon before coming to the farm, but the peace and quiet of the farm gave me an opportunity to focus on a more intimate relationship with the Lord. Most days I found myself praying, talking to God. And sometimes, I even felt like singing when I was feeding some of the cattle. In the evenings one of the guards would release me out the back gate to walk down to the barns alone so I could feed grain to the cattle. No one else was around, so I felt free to do this, but I got some strange looks from the steers when I started to sing. And in the beauty of the wilderness I often saw deer in the fields. I was so thankful for the air I could breathe here, and simple freedoms, even if only for a short time. There was a joy in my heart that only God could put there.

It had been over two and a half years since I had left MCF in Muskegon. One of the miracles of that time was that Judy was still alive and fighting cancer back in Indiana. We continued our correspondence and phone calls and we developed a relationship that we had never had before that was built on Christ. God had used me to encourage and minister to her in the fight against cancer. She had beaten the odds and shocked the doctors by surviving three brain surgeries to remove tumors. She was a tiny woman and God had given her a will and determination to never give up. I know that it was because of the faith she had in Jesus that God continued to give her life. I also continued to believe with her for the miracle healing power He had poured into her and I thanked God.

The year 1998 was the last for me at the farm. Many things began to change. The department of corrections was changing the way they operated, taking away many privileges, and making everything appear more like prison. Even trustee division and the Mangum Farm became affected. Workers came out to start running razor wire across the top of the fence line, and they began installing steel bars on the windows of the barracks. Massive shakedowns took place with teams of guards going through the main prison, and then coming out to the farm, looking for contraband and weapons. There were none at the farm. Because of the changes inmates lost the privileges to receive personal clothing, except for undergarments. At the farm everyone regularly wore prison blues, and only wore street clothing when going to the prison for a visit. The harsh reality of prison life was reaching out in every level of confinement. Many of us had to send property home that was no longer allowed. Even the weight room facility we had underwent a major change. All free weights were removed and a single machine installed. One of our most prized privileges was gone.

By fall the atmosphere of the prison system became even bitterer. I had developed a friendship with one of the men who was between 45 and 50. I didn't consider him a brother in Christ, but I had spoken to him about the Lord. I believe that God was tugging at his heart, and he was excited because he was going to be released soon and going home. He spoke of his wife and his deep love for her. I could see there was great joy in his eyes as he talked about her and finally going home. Three days later, on a Saturday afternoon, I stood with other inmates, watching in shock as officers worked on his body to revive him. He had been exercising in the yard outside the barracks, and went to sit on a picnic bench with some of the other men when he collapsed. The men acted quickly to get the officers on duty. As I stood there watching his lifeless body never regain consciousness I became numb inside, asking God how could this happen, and why. It seemed like a waste that his life would end this way, and painful for what his wife would suffer.

The numbness I felt inside that day was something I had been carrying with me since April. It was during that month that Judy died. The cancer had finally overtaken her body and the battle she had fought for almost three years was over. My heart was broken. There was a part of me that was empty after her death, and thinking that there could never be anyone for me I truly believed that I would never marry. But one thing I learned as a Christian is that when we give our lives to Christ He changes the desires of our hearts. That is exactly what happened to me. All the years of my life before I was saved I was a womanizer like my father. Even though I had been in relationships here and there I was never committed to one woman. I had acted in the same manner with Judy, and it wasn't until many years in prison that I began to have the desire to have a relationship with her alone, a relationship based on real love. I had never known it before because my motives were always selfish. But when God changed my heart I learned that real love is self-sacrifice. I was no longer the person who mattered most. It was the other person. We had found something new together through Christ and had talked about marriage after I got out of prison. Now there was no future with her. My life and the future to come were going to be determined by God. For by Him alone I was going to receive strength and have the courage I needed to go on.

For the seven years now that I had been incarcerated I learned that the pain I had brought upon my family, and that I suffered personally, pushed me closer to God and deeper into His Word. It was a means by which He graciously shaped me to be like His Son, gradually giving me the compassion, contentment, tranquility, and courage I longed and prayed for. Without that pain, I would not become all that God wanted me to be. His strength shined brightest in me through my human weakness. God allowed me to be set apart to receive instruction through suffering and pain. As I patiently endured this training God turned my trials into a blessing. He used it to draw me close to His heart and into His Word, teaching me the lessons He intended for me to learn, and using it to bestow His grace upon me. God was making me something much better than I ever thought possible.

Chapter 11

As the end of the year drew near and the snow began to fall I became eligible and was approved for community placement at the correctional center in Grand Rapids, a facility where non-violent prisoners were sent to begin a transition to parole. It was here that this period of adjustment would begin to take place for me. The center was no longer the previous rundown motel where I had gone years earlier. It was a new facility built of brick and thick unbreakable windows, with security cameras and electronic doors. It was a state of the art facility designed for security.

The main lobby had an officer station situated behind thick glass where inmates signed in and out of the building. There were offices down an adjoining hallway on one side, a holding cell and office to the rear of the officer station, and a hallway on the opposite side where a classroom was located for orientation and a wing with rooms for inmates. There was also a mess hall for meals across the hallway.

There were two additional floors, with officer stations in the middle of each floor. The floors were L-shaped to give officers a complete view of each hallway for monitoring prisoner movement, with showers and restrooms located behind the officer station. The rooms were constructed of blocks, with steel doors. Inmates were referred to as *Residents* and each was given a key to the room they shared with another person. Staff had keys to all rooms for daily inspections and taking count for all residents who were not signed out to work, attend classes, or fulfill responsibilities on work crews that were staffed by a corrections officer. The third floor of the corrections center was reserved for female prisoners.

The rules and regulations of the corrections center had become extremely strict, in keeping with the changes the Department of Corrections (DOC) had been making. No longer was there the kind of freedom of movement there had been in years past. The DOC had established a zero tolerance policy. As a regular practice the officers on duty checked on prisoners who had signed out for jobs or family visits to ensure they were going where they were supposed to. Another strict rule was the enforcement of time stipulations. If inmates returned to the center one minute late from a job, visit, church, or job search they were immediately placed into custody in the holding cell and charged with attempted escape. The prisoner was then transferred to the local county jail pending a hearing on the charge, and most often returned to prison where they remained until parole.

Prisoners were allowed to select one location for visits, usually a family member's home, where they would eventually parole to. A representative of the DOC visited the home first before the location was approved. At first I had selected my sister's home, which was in a rural area about 20 minutes south of the downtown area. Here I was able to go on Saturdays and Sundays and spend four hours each day after I had established a full-time job. For the initial first two weeks of orientation I was permitted to go for one day.

I arrived in Grand Rapids on a cold snowy December evening about a week before Christmas in 1998. An officer from the corrections center arrived with a van and we were all taken to the center. After arrival we were fed and taken to the classroom in the building for an orientation meeting, where we were informed of the zero tolerance policy, and that there were no exceptions whatsoever. After the meeting my mother had stopped at the center, and I was allowed to visit with her for a short time. She had brought me clothing and some money. I was overjoyed to see her after the long journey, and told her I would call as soon as I learned more details about whether I would be permitted to spend Christmas with the family. The first two weeks I spent exclusively in the center working in the mess hall, and on work crews with a corrections officer. Then I was allowed to search for a job.

I was assigned to a room where I was assigned to live with another inmate. The next morning I woke up at 4:30 and dressed to report for work in the mess hall. A civilian worker assigned inmates different tasks and they took care of cleaning and helping with meal preparation and serving the other residents of the facility. During the next two weeks my routine was to report early each morning, working until breakfast had been served, then report again before lunch to help with the noon meal for residents who were not working during the day. Afternoons I was assigned under the supervision of a corrections officer. With the December snow falling quickly I spent much time on the work crew shoveling snow outside the facility.

My home placement at my sister's residence had been approved the first week, and I learned by Thursday that I was going to be able to spend a few hours with her the next day which was Christmas. My sister showed up to pick me up early afternoon on Christmas day. It was the first time I had seen her in person in a few years. We had spoken by phone while I was in northern Michigan, but I had not seen her since I was at Muskegon.

This was the first Christmas I was going to spend with my family in eight years, and it was the first time I had the freedom to travel in a vehicle in public with someone other than a prison employee. I was very timid at seeing the outside world, like a lost woodland creature that wandered into the city by mistake. The world looked completely different to me, as if I had entered into it for the first time in my life.

That morning in the car my sister handed me a Christmas card. As I opened it and looked inside I broke down and wept. It was something very precious, and personal, and it touched my heart. As I held my sister's hand, tears continued to flow down my cheeks. It was a bittersweet feeling to have lost all those years and yet to have gained so much through Christ. I was so thankful for that Christmas. For me it was a gift from God to spend that time with my family, to share a meal, and give thanks to God. I was overwhelmed, and I was happy to be with all of them for the first time in such a long time.

God showed me how precious life is, and how each moment should be experienced with an attitude of thanksgiving.

After two weeks I was permitted to begin searching for a job. One of the requirements for residents to have the privilege of home weekend visits was maintaining steady employment, and completing work duty in the center for a few hours each week. On my first day of job hunting my mother picked me up. I had to document each business I visited, each person I spoke with, and the time of day I arrived and left the business. Before leaving the center I had spoken to other men who had found jobs in factories nearby, and my priority was to find any job available.

That first day searching I found a job at a local factory within walking distance of the center about a mile away. I continued to rise early each morning at 4:30 and volunteered to work in the mess hall before going to work. I had completed my requirement to work in the mess hall the first two weeks I was at the center and I enjoyed it, and volunteering my time kept me busy while I was there. I would sign out of the building at 6:30 and walk to work, taking a bag lunch with me. Afterwards I returned directly to the facility. About a month later I found a job working in another factory a bit closer to the center, which paid a bit more. A portion of my earnings each week went to pay for rent, which was a requirement for all residents.

On weekends my sister or brother-in-law picked me up for home visits, and on Sundays my mother picked me up to go to church with her. My life as a Christian gave me the gift of true fellowship with my mother. It was no longer her ministering to a son that didn't want to listen. It was now a relationship, and fellowship through Christ. The small Pentecostal church my mother had attended in Wyoming, Michigan for years was a group of loving and giving Christian people. No longer did I go with her as an observer. I became a participant. These people were passionate about worshipping God in prayer and in singing praises. During the many weeks I had been going with my mother God opened my eyes to reveal to me how pleased He is with the praise and worship of his people. As I looked at others, with hands lifted, tears of joy on their faces, I saw the intimacy that they were experiencing with God. I wanted to have that more than ever, and as I sought to touch and see the face of God in my life He drew me into a more intimate relationship with Him.

I realized more and more each day that I could do nothing without Christ, and a part of me feared the world when I left the confinement of the center. Every day walking to and from work I prayed. I never wanted to return to the life I had once lived, or to ever become the prideful person I once was. Possessions became unimportant to me. A part of me was lonely and longing for a relationship as well.

God was drawing me nearer to Him and changing my heart even more since I had left the confines of prison. All of my life I had several relationships with women, but I had never married. I saw marriage as a failure because of my parent's marriage and divorce. I had told myself most all of my life that I would never get married. My mother had now been remarried to my step-father for almost 30 years, and their example showed me that marriage was more than a certificate and vows. It was a covenant established by God, and designed by him. And now God was changing the desires of my heart, and I began to long for one special person, one woman that God would bring into my life. When Judy died while I was in prison I thought that she was the only one who could fill that void, but God continued to work on my heart and that part of me that longed for someone only God could bring into my life.

By the spring of 1999 I had been working a new job at a steel supply company in Grand Rapids. It was farther across town from the center, and I had been taking the city bus to work until I was able to buy a bicycle and ride to work. I enjoyed the exercise and the freedom. I was working fifty to sixty hours a week at the steel supply company, and had started another job working Friday and Saturday evening's waiting tables at a restaurant in one of the local hotels. I was working a lot, which kept me out of the center, and at the same time I was being financially blessed. I had been tithing since prison. My mother had taught me the importance of giving back to God what he had already blessed me with, and it seemed like the more I gave the more I got blessed.

In July I was called in to see one of the counselors at the center and informed that I was eligible to be placed at home on tether. My sister was in the process of selling her home, and so I requested placement at my mother's home. Within a week it was approved and a device installed in the house. An electronic bracelet was placed on my ankle and a schedule setup for me to come and go from the house to attend work. I was also allotted time on Sundays to attend church. I was required to report one day each week to a counselor at the center regarding my job status and to provide him with my paycheck earnings. I was also frequently tested for drugs, which was a normal procedure done on all residents and those living on tether.

My mother and step-father Larry welcomed me home with love and support. I began to develop a closer relationship with my step-father, which was something I never established in years past. He had been concerned because I had come to live with them ten years earlier under similar circumstances, and later on my mother was hurt because of my actions. Pa (my step-father) wanted to protect my mother. But the difference in my life was that I was not living for myself anymore, but for Christ. He recognized that, and even though in the back of his mind there may have been some worry, I know that over time his fears subsided.

My dear mother treated me like the *Prodigal Son* that returned home. She would always have dinner waiting for me when I got home from work, ask if I needed anything, and shower me with love. I don't think I could ever praise God enough for giving me such a mother that exemplifies Christ in every area of her life. She has always had the most loving and giving heart of anyone I ever knew. She has always had the heart of a servant.

Over the course of the months I lived with Mom and Pa, I began to pray each night with my mother. She would come downstairs to my room and kneel with me on the floor to pray. Then she would return upstairs to pray with Pa before they turned in for the night. Those prayers became very special to me. I'm sure that each night when my dear mother prayed with Pa afterwards they were praying for me as well.

God continued changing the desires of my heart, and I longed for one special woman in my life. In the previous months I had been "shopping," as I like to put it, looking for what I thought was the perfect woman for me. It didn't occur to me at the time that trying to find what I thought I needed was the wrong way to go about it.

So I began to pray, and asked God to bring one woman into my life, chosen by Him. There was a part of me that felt empty, and after I prayed I knew I had to rely on God, and His timing, for the desires of my heart to be met.

God used that time to demonstrate his love for me. During this time of transition for me God spoke to me through His Word and through books. I felt the depth and magnitude of His love in a way that I had never experienced before. It made me realize that God loves me more than anyone ever had or ever could, and that His love never ends. As I look back I realize that God was preparing me and teaching me how to love as He does. I began to seek God on a greater level than I ever had in my life in prison. I longed to see His face and to hear His voice. I began to read a book called *Jesus Loves Me* by H.L. Roush, Sr. As I read through the pages I began to see and feel the depth of His love for me. I had never understood real love, or its purpose. In one of the passages I saw how God had used so many different people over the course of the last 7-8 years of my life to touch me with the love of Jesus. Roush writes,

> *"Real love must contact others in some perceptible way. Jesus' love for others must be realized through some personal touch with reality; for if anyone is to know that Jesus loves them, someone must bring Jesus and His love to them in life. You are where you are, that Jesus might be there. He will walk the dusty roads of life as He did the Emmaus road, disguised through you as a stranger, to overtake those who are discouraged, afraid, and miserable. He will talk with them through you, become their friend, break bread with them and reveal Himself through your heart, that their hearts might be set ablaze with love Himself. Their eyes will be opened and they will see that it was Jesus loving them all the time, not you."[1]*

Those words spoke to my heart to show me Jesus in my mother loving and praying for me all those years, Chaplain Bob Hall and his wife Jamie ministering and loving me through Christ, and Richard Amo in the prison yard, shining with the light and love of Christ.

Jesus was in all these people, and others, bringing me the hope and peace that I had never known before.

As I grew spiritually in my relationship with God He began to tug at my heart, leading me down the path he wanted me to follow. I had been attending my mother's church for some time, and visiting another church in Grandville, Michigan. The pastor there was Duane VanderKlok. I had listened to his tapes while I was in prison, and seen his television ministry *Walking By Faith.* After I visited Resurrection Life Church, I felt God telling me more and more that this was where He wanted me to be. My mother was very protective of me, and wanted to make sure I was attending a *spirit-filled* church where the love and power of Christ was present. I assured her it was, and over the course of time she attended with me a few times to visit.

The praise and worship at Resurrection Life was powerful, and I always felt the presence of the Holy Spirit. For years I had not fully understood praise and worship at the beginning of church services, and when I was not serving God I looked at it as a waste of time, as some sort of ritual. When the light went off in my head one day during the worship at my mother's church I realized that this was more important than anything else. As I poured out my heart to God with hands lifted high during these wonderful times of praise I felt God's Holy Spirit filling me on the inside. The Bible says that God inhabits the praises of His people. As I continued to attend the church in Grandville I knew in my heart that this was where God intended for me to be at this time in my life.

Pastor Duane had a great gift for teaching God's Word, and his style of teaching brought the Bible to life for me in a new way, as an instruction manual, a guide for living. I had never considered or realized that every aspect of living our lives is taught by God's Word. Whether it is marriage, financial matters, or relationships, the Bible is a foundation for living our lives. It is a blueprint given to us by God. Pastor Duane's practical applications to the Word gave me a common sense understanding of the Bible that I had never considered before. After all the years of studying the Bible in prison, and knowing the scriptures, I didn't stop to think about applying the principles to every area of my life. As a common practice I began to do just that, and pray about every situation in my life, giving it over to God.

Chapter 12

On December 15, 1999 I was approved for parole and the tether removed from my ankle. The monitoring device in my mother's home was also removed. Mom and Pa encouraged me to stay with them, and while living at home they helped me purchase a used vehicle to drive to and from work. It had been eight years since I drove a car on a public road so I had to take a road test and a written test to receive my license. I continued to work two jobs, and offered to pay rent, but my parents refused because they wanted me to have plenty of money saved to get a place to live and provide for whatever needs I might have in the future.

I continued to stay close to home, and to my parents during this new transition. I had been given much more freedom now, which required even more responsibility on my part. I had applied to go back to college because I had a desire to find a career doing something I enjoyed. I already had a bachelor's degree in Criminal Justice, but obviously I was not going to pursue a career in law enforcement. I had been thinking for a long time of looking at a career working with computers since I had taken classes in prison and caught on quickly.

I was accepted to attend Davenport University in Grand Rapids, a business college that also had a degree program in computer technology. I decided to pursue a degree in Network Engineering, which would also be a business degree. I purchased a new computer and in January I began college.

It was over 20 years since I had attended college, and in many ways it was intimidating and uncomfortable for me at first. I was 43 years old, among mostly younger people just out of high school, but fortunately there were some older business people that took classes and I didn't feel too out of place. I knew I was doing the right thing though, and that I was supposed to be here. I had prayed about it for months, and had even postponed attending six months earlier because I felt God telling me it wasn't time yet, until now.

When I had attended college the first time after high school I was not a devoted student. I was more interested in drinking beer with my football friends and chasing girls. I felt at a great disadvantage now, but I was determined that with God's help I could get through this. I carried with me in my pocket a small business card wallet, with an inscription on the front, *"I can do all things through Christ who strengthens me." (Philippians 4:13).* For the next few years, and until my graduation, I continued to carry it, and take it out many times to look at it and remind myself that I could do all things through Christ who gave me strength.

That month, and that year, God began to make many wonderful things happen. One of the bubbliest people I ever met was a gal named Michelle Kakabaker. Just pronouncing her name was a mouthful. I had seen her before at services because she sang on the praise and worship team at Resurrection Life Church. She had a beautiful and powerful soprano voice. I attended a service with a male friend and Michelle approached us to introduce herself and tell us about the singles meetings. I had a desire to get more involved at my church, and began attending the meetings.

I got involved in the singles group to meet others from my church and develop some new friendships. I didn't plan to look for a relationship with any of the single women, and what I didn't expect was meeting my future wife. Michelle had invited me to a gathering at her home on a Friday evening where others from the church singles group would also be attending. I was the first person to arrive, and was talking with Michelle about music, explaining how I had done much singing in high school and college. She asked me to sing, so I started singing a song by Stephen Curtis Chapman, *(Be Still And Know That He Is God)*. At that very moment Lorie, my future wife walked in. I finished singing and Michelle introduced Lorie to me. Other guests had not arrived yet, so we began to talk. Well, we ended up talking for three hours straight. Looking back I don't even remember what we talked about, but it must have been everything! I did find out that she was divorced, had a 15 year-old daughter at home, and she also attended the same church. We exchanged stories about church, different events there, and couldn't figure out how we had never met before. Lorie was a very attractive woman, tall with long dark hair, but what I remembered most about her was her beautiful smile. That night as we left to head home I walked her to her car and asked her if she would meet me Sunday morning at church and sit with me. She said yes and I went home very excited.

Something in me stirred that night, and before I climbed into bed I prayed, asking God if this could be the one He had chosen for me. Even God must have thought I was crazy to ask such a question just a few hours after meeting this woman, but my heart was stirring.

That Sunday morning I arrived at church and waited for Lorie in the foyer, but she didn't show. I assumed something must have come up and she couldn't make it. I called her later that day at home to see if everything was okay and she told me she was unable to get her car started that morning. The problem had been fixed so we planned to meet at church for the evening service. That evening I went back to church for service and got there early. I always preferred to arrive early to talk to people, and I ran into Michelle. I asked her if she had seen Lorie and she said no. Then the funniest thing happened. Lorie came running up to Michelle, staring her in the face, exclaiming, *"Have you seen John? Have you seen him?"* I'm standing there two feet away and I begin waving, *"Hello! I'm right here!"* So that was the hilarious beginning of our courtship.

I took every opportunity to talk with Lorie on the phone at night after work, or stopped at her home to visit when I didn't have class in the evening. I had met her daughter Jessica and we hit it off very well. The three of us would spend a lot of time together, worshipping and attending church, laughing at their home playing games, and eating ice cream.

I had also shared with Lorie my past, and she found it hard to believe that I was a convicted felon. She recognized in me how much

I loved Christ. For me it was a testimony of Him living in me, and showing the truth of God's Word in *2 Corinthians* 5:17 that says *"if any man be in Christ he is a new creation..."*

On March 3, which was Lorie's birthday, I took her out for dinner to the restaurant where I had been working on weekends. I had quit earlier in the year because I was going to school, and my full-time job at the steel supply company kept me quite busy. One of the waitresses I had worked with waited on us and I introduced her to Lorie. After she took our order and went to the kitchen I pulled out a small gift box for Lorie to open. It was a diamond ring. Her eyes got huge as she opened the box. I expressed my love for her and asked her to marry me. Joyfully she said yes, and that night we went to share the news and show the ring to family. We later tentatively set a wedding date for August.

Later that month I traveled with Lorie to Florida to meet her parents. They were retired and living in Port Charlotte. I had never met them before and thought it would be proper for them to meet me. I was a bit old fashioned as well, and wanted to ask her parents to bless our marriage. Her father had been in the plumbing and heating business for years. He had also been a marine, having served in the Korean War. He was a bit skeptical of me at first, but Lorie's mother welcomed me with open arms. When we shared that we were getting married Lorie's mother was very excited, while her father was reserved. We had an enjoyable time with them and talked about the Lord. Both Lorie's parents were Christians and they invited us to their church while there. That was the beginning of my relationship with them, which grew during the years of my marriage to Lorie. We did not tell them about my past or that I had been a convicted felon. Lorie and I decided it would be better not to tell them. Their first impression of me was based on what they learned on our initial visit. About five years later I decided to tell them the story of my life after I felt God speaking to my heart and telling me it was time.

By the second week of April I asked Lorie to elope with me, but not to tell her daughter Jessica because telling her would be like telling everyone we knew. We wanted to surprise everyone. Only God can make the impossible become possible, and within a week we attended a class and received the marriage certificate, arranged for a wedding dress and tuxedo, and picked out our rings. I called Chaplain Bob and his wife Jamie to ask them where they would be on April 15, which was a Saturday. I had expected them to be in Traverse City, and planned on taking Lorie there. But Bob and Jamie had plans to visit a man at a prison facility near Saginaw that weekend, so I told them we would meet them there. On Friday Lorie stopped at my parent's home with Jessica and I discreetly packed a tuxedo in the trunk as Lorie and Jessica spoke to my step-father. We had told my parents and Jessica that we were going to Saginaw for the weekend to visit Bob and Jamie. My mother had gone to a church retreat for the weekend so she wasn't home at the time.

Before we drove to Saginaw we stopped at a local park to take some engagement photos, but Jessica still did not know what was going on. She knew we were engaged, but thought we had planned to get married in August. Finally on the road, about halfway there, we told her we were going to Saginaw to get married. She thought we were kidding with her, until we arrived at the hotel and brought the wedding gown into the hotel. But reality didn't set in until morning.

Jessica and Lorie shared the adjoining room next to mine, and the next morning they began to get ready. I had been on the phone with Bob and Jamie trying to locate a public location for a wedding. We arranged to meet at the Bay City State Park on Saginaw Bay. My best man Rick arrived that morning, and I informed him of the plans. After leaving the hotel we met Bob and Jamie at their hotel. The men went on ahead to the state park, and entering the gate there was not much traffic. We stopped at the gate, and I asked the park ranger if it was okay to have a wedding in the park. He was a young fellow, and his response was *"Cool!"* Well, we knew that meant yes, and we found a beautiful open spot near the beach. Soon after we saw Jamie's car pulling in, and out climbed the women. Lorie looked like a princess. I know that the reality of it all suddenly hit Jessica as we setup and proceeded to begin the ceremony, and she began to cry nonstop. I almost felt like we were starting a funeral, but her tears were joyful ones for her mother.

So we began our lives together that day. It was four months since I had met Lorie, but I believed in my heart that God brought her into my life at the time he had established. Over 40 years of my life I had never planned on marriage, but God changed my heart, and I've been thankful ever since for a godly and loving wife.

Lorie was truly a gift from God to me. Almost two years before I met her Judy died from cancer and there was a void in me that I did not think could ever be filled. When God changed the desires of my heart after coming home to live a life of freedom I had no idea what He had in store for me. I learned that God not only meets our needs and fulfills our desires, but He does it above and beyond what we could ever imagine. That is what God did when He brought Lorie into my life. She is much more than my wife and my partner. She is in fact the love of my life and my best friend.

After we returned home and shared the news with my parents and the rest of the family we promised to hold a ceremony again in August so that we could celebrate our marriage with family and friends. For the next few months we began planning as we moved into a beautiful farm house on four acres of land.

Life for me changed beyond measure. The only two females I had ever lived with before were my mother and sister. Now I had a wife and a daughter, and I began to learn how to be a husband and a father. I learned that at times it was work, and challenging, but with God's guidance (and grace) it gave me great joy.

In late August we had diligently been planning the wedding for family and friends to be a part of. We decided to have it on our property behind the house. We had a huge back yard and a separate driveway beyond the house for additional traffic and parking. My parents provided a large outdoor tent for our guests, and we had also arranged for caterers and music. The best part of all this was the people who would come to share in our joy that day.

I like to share this story because it demonstrates how God can change the world. My dear friend Richard Amo, who had been my spiritual father and brother in Christ in prison 9 years earlier, came that day to the wedding. As I had shared earlier, Richard was serving two natural back to back life sentences with no chance of parole. By law in Michigan life sentences are automatically appealed. His convictions were appealed, and an attorney was appointed by the court to represent him. Richard had never intended to appeal his convictions, and had planned to spend the rest of his life in prison. By early 1998 the Court of Appeals overturned his convictions, and the prosecutor offered him a plea bargain for a reduced charge. On the day of sentencing Richard was given the opportunity to speak, and for the first time in his life he spoke in a courtroom about how Christ had changed his life. When it was all over the judge sentenced Richard to "time served."

Richard was not immediately discharged because the federal authorities had pending charges they had been holding for selling guns to Columbian drug runners. He had already been incarcerated almost ten years. Another plea bargain was arranged and Richard was released from federal custody with time served within the same year. He had resigned himself to spend the rest of his life in prison, but God had other plans for him. Seeing Richard again in August of 2000 was a pure joy for me. It was our first face-to-face meeting after prison. I had not seen him in several years. Now on this summer day in August he came to celebrate my marriage. What a joy it was to see him again in person, free, and giving him a hug. Since that day we continued to exchange letters, cards, and phone calls. Richard had been serving in a ministry in St. Claire Shores, Michigan, and a few years later he moved to Florida to be close to his children and grandchildren. He then began to go into Florida prisons to minister to men. The ministry that Richard went to work for was run by Pastor Steve Upshur who had led Richard to Christ about ten years earlier in the Macomb County Jail. Peacemaker International was the ministry founded by Pastor Steve. It became a very important part of Richard Amo's life and he dedicated it to serving the Lord.

(Richard Amo – After his release living in Florida)

I was also overjoyed to see my Uncle Jim and Aunt Rose come that day. They had traveled the long trip from the Upper Peninsula to come and celebrate this special day with Lorie and me. After having developed a relationship through their many visits to the prison at Marquette it was even more special for them to come and be with us. They had become precious family to me like so many and it was truly a great honor for me to share this day with them.

That year brought many firsts for me, and I considered each of them a gift from God. Life had become more precious to me than ever before, and God continued to bring people into my life that had an impact on my future. I've learned that marriage can have struggles and that it takes work, but the rewards far outweigh the negative, especially when God is at the head of the marriage. Lorie supported me through going to college again for the first three and a half years of our marriage. She has been my cheerleader, or as I refer to her, my biggest fan. God has not only blessed our marriage, but He has strengthened it and taught me more than I ever knew about love and sacrifice. I've learned that marriage was designed by God to never be broken. It is a covenant established by Him between a man and a woman. Our faith and our commitment to serving the Lord has strengthened our marriage and made it better with each passing day.

Chapter 13

My private life was very happy. I was blessed to have a home life with Lorie and Jessica loving me and supporting me in all I did at college and in my work. Family was very important to me. God had shown me how precious life is and every day I valued the time we spent together. It was the first family of my own that I ever had, and all of us especially enjoyed family get-together's with our extended families.

We began a new family tradition in the spring of 2000 when we invited my parents, my sister and her grown children, along with Lorie's brother's and sisters, their children, and Lorie's parents for Father's Day. Everyone brought food and we set up tents, tables and chairs. Lorie and I supplied the hot dogs and hamburgers. I think the best part was when our families gathered together to pray the first time. Everyone, including the children, formed a circle in the yard and we held hands. I led the prayer and gave thanks to God for the time He gave us together. Then we enjoyed a picnic together and played outdoor games in the yard. It was an opportunity for us to bring both sides of our family together. We look forward to these times together to help us build relationships on both sides of the family.

One of the things that Lorie and I agreed upon when we got married was not to tell Jessica or her family about my felony convictions and that I was on parole. We trusted that God would determine the right time for sharing such information about my past. My immediate family knew and they agreed that it was best not to share my history.

In the meantime I continued to focus on my studies while attending night school, and working full time. That same year I had also changed jobs, taking a position with a company that sold tax and accounting products, including software. I had an opportunity and took a job providing technical support for their tax accounting software. During the application process I had to provide information regarding my convictions, which was kept confidential, and I began my new job as a technical support specialist in the fall. With all the changes that had been taking place in my life God had also been working on my heart again. I have two half-brothers, Ben and Randy that lived in the Grand Rapids area and I had not seen them in years. God had put it on my heart to develop a relationship with them. I contacted them and invited them and their wives to our home for dinner on a Friday evening. That evening after dinner while the women were visiting I took some time with my brothers and shared with them how Christ had changed my life. They had not seen me since before I had been a police officer, and when I spoke to them that night they quietly listened as I talked about the Lord, and how he had changed me. My brother Ben and his wife Michelle were believers, and Randy's wife Shelly was a believer as well, but not Randy. Even so, we began a relationship as brothers, and once in awhile we get together socially.

I had not seen my natural father for almost ten years now, and at that time he was working in a factory that produced jet engine parts. My brother Randy worked there too, and Ben had his own auto repair business. Both of them saw our father regularly, and when I asked about him they told me that he had not changed. He lived his life alone, after having been divorced again years earlier from their mother. His lifestyle was working and drinking. He had little or no money.

I made no effort at that time in my life to contact my father. In my heart I had forgiven him for the past, and I had no connection with him. He had not been a part of my life, and at that time I did not feel a need or a reason to get in touch with him. I had a new life now, and a wife and daughter to take care of.

I continued to focus on my schooling and work, and enjoying the new life God gave me with Lorie and Jessica. I also maintained my spiritual relationship with others who had impacted my life, like Chaplain Bob and Jamie, Richard Amo, and a couple of men I had known in prison as brothers in Christ. Those relationships were very important to me.

I desired to receive all I could from God, and continued to receive solid teaching from our church. My wife Lorie also exposed me to some teaching that I had not heard before or read about. I exercised on a regular basis in the family room, and sometimes I would have the television on. If I left the room momentarily and came back Lorie would sometimes change the channel to Christian television. I was not used to watching Christian programming, and at first I thought my wife was trying to force feed me, which I resented. I would change the channel, but sooner or later Christian programming would come on again. One day I saw and heard this woman speaking. She was talking like a preacher, and her speaking was forceful. At first I didn't care to listen to this woman, which was probably a pride issue, but after I heard her speak a few times I realized that God was using her to speak to my heart. Her name was Joyce Meyer. I began to listen to her regularly, and listen to her tapes. I had heard Joyce's testimony about her childhood, and the pain she had endured from her father. Her suffering was worse than mine. But I was able to relate to her on a certain level because of our past. Her teaching became a part of my life. I had no idea at the time that in a few years some of her books would play a role in the greatest healing of my life.

About a year after Lorie and I had been married I began to feel the Holy Spirit tugging on me to speak to my step-daughter Jessica and tell her about my past. Lorie and I had spoken about it on previous occasions, and had sensed that the timing was not right, until now. I still had less than a year to serve on parole, and I reported to my parole officer once a month to report my earnings and talk about my progress. The parole office was only about two miles from our home, and my parole officer had stopped at the house at least twice to check up on me. He had never announced himself as my parole officer, but Lorie knew, and Jessica just thought it was one of my old friends looking for me. I felt that Jessica was able to handle it, and I sat down with her and told her about my past as a fallen police officer, my life of crime, and how Christ came into my life and changed me. Her response was even better than I expected. She loved me and respected me even more. We had developed a great deal of trust, and she looked at me sharing this part of my life with her as something sacred.

As a practice I did not tell people about my past if they didn't already know. Because of the way that some people reacted when they found out my criminal history I was even more guarded about telling people. I had not shared this information with people from my church either, except Pastor Duane VanderKlok. The summer of 2000 I had met him at a gathering on a Wednesday evening in the youth room at church and began talking to him. I knew he was into physical fitness and I started talking to him about weightlifting. He asked me if I wanted to join him for lunch sometime, and I had Lorie set it up with his secretary a week later. He didn't know anything about me at the time, since we had just met. His oldest son Joshua went with us, and when Pastor Duane asked me to tell him about myself I started talking and didn't stop until I had told him about my past as a police officer, a felon, and a transformed person. I felt later that perhaps I shouldn't have shared so much. He may not even remember that day now as I do, but I found out that people generally form opinions on a first meeting based on what they see and hear. I found this to be true with Christians too. God teaches us not to judge, but human nature has a way of taking a different course at times. I became very careful about sharing my past with anyone until I felt that it was necessary, or because God had spoken to my heart about it.

About one and a half years into our marriage my wife continued to be patient as I attended night classes and worked toward my degree. Our lives were always very busy and full. After the September 11, 2001 attacks on the World Trade Center in New York City we saw the world in a different context that affected our future as well. By spring of the following year I lost my job. Like many companies that were affected economically after the terrorist's attacks the company I worked for began to downsize. As a result my entire division was eliminated and the jobs moved to another state. Everyone, including my manager, was terminated.

I had about 30 days to find another job before leaving the company. I prepared a resume and began emailing it to different people, including the head faculty of the computer technology program at Davenport University. It had been just a few days and I received a reply about a possible job opportunity with one of the intermediate school districts. The job was working as a Technology Services Specialist for the summer. It was the end of May and the job was to begin in June. My resume had been forwarded to the director of technology and within a few days I received a call for an interview. After the initial interview I felt very comfortable and confident about possibly getting the job. If hired I would be working in the main administration building, providing computer hardware and software support for the network. Soon after the interview I was hired and began my new job. My past had not been brought up, and as a practice I did not volunteer it unless it was required. This was a summer job anyway, and I only expected to work for the intermediate school district (ISD) throughout the summer months.

The job turned out to be fantastic, and I developed a wonderful working relationship with my supervisor, who was at the time the network administrator. It turned out that she was a Christian, and on many mornings before starting work, or during the course of the work day when we had a break, we would talk about the Lord. I grew to enjoy this job more than any I had ever had, and found it very rewarding. I looked forward to going to work each day and shared with my wife Lorie how much I liked my new job. She had come to my workplace and met my supervisor and other co-workers. It was a positive atmosphere, and everyone worked together very well.

By the end of August the director of technology called me into her office and offered to extend my stay for a couple more months. The pay was good, and I was happy to have work there as long as I could. She also told me confidentially that they were considering whether to create a permanent position, and inquired if I would be interested. I told her I would be, and within the next two months they posted an opening for the job. I applied, and had to interview with a panel of three people. I went through three different interviews before they offered me the position. I was ecstatic, and shared the news with my wife.

In the meantime Lorie and I had been looking to purchase a new home. We had hoped to buy the home we were leasing since we got married, but the owner had decided that he wanted to move into the home and start his own family. He was a young man and we understood. We were thankful for the time we were able to live there.

We had been looking for a couple of months, since July, when Lorie had found a beautiful home on a lake about 30 miles north of Grand Rapids. We looked at it in early September, prayed about it, and made an offer. We felt that this was the home God had intended for us to have. The owners accepted our offer, and by mid-September we closed on the house. The deal provided that we would take possession at the end of October. Everything seemed to be going perfect, and we began to get ready for the move. In the meantime I prepared for my job status to change to a permanent employee at the beginning of August.

The last couple of weeks of September the Holy Sprit began to speak to my heart again. Even though I had been working for the intermediate school district for five months now and had established trust with them, they still did not know about my past. Their policy was to conduct a background check with the state police on all permanent employees. I began to struggle with this and talked to my wife about it. One part of me argued that I was here because God had blessed me, and I had nothing to worry about. I also spoke to my mother about it, and although she would not tell me what she thought I should do, she began to pray about it. I called Chaplain Bob and his wife Jamie, and their response was the same. I was almost hoping that someone would tell me what to do.

On a Tuesday morning I determined that I needed to talk to the director of technology and tell her about my past before I started the permanent job. It wasn't a matter of conscience. It was the Holy Spirit speaking to my heart, and I knew that doing this was the right thing. That morning I went into the director's office, sat down, and explained to her that when I took the initial job there I thought it would only be temporary. I had no idea that it would turn into something permanent. I told her that I thought she should know some things about my background before I started the permanent position. I proceeded to tell her about my past as a police officer, a convicted felon, and how Christ had changed my life. I didn't quite know what to expect, and she told me she would have to do some checking and get back to me later. I went about my daily routine as normal. By early afternoon I was paged and reported to the director. She had me follow her to human resources. The two of us went into the office, and within a few minutes I was told that I was being let go by the human resources director. Apparently the final decision had been made by the superintendent, and his decision was to terminate me. All of the hard work and dedication I had demonstrated during that time felt meaningless. I was also told that I had to leave the property immediately. As I left the director accompanied me to my desk so I could gather a few things, and she walked me to the back door of the building. She told me she was sorry, and gave me a hug. She was a dear lady, and I knew she felt horrible about the entire situation. As I walked to my car and got in I felt numb, like I had been kicked in the stomach and my heart ripped out.

It was still early afternoon when I went home. As soon as Lorie saw me she knew something was wrong. When I told her what happened we both began to cry, finding it difficult to understand. For the first time since we married my past had become an issue.

The following day I received an email from my supervisor at the ISD. She had not been there the previous day when all the events unfolded, but she had heard the story. She said to me that I was a man of integrity, something no one had ever said to me before. It was consolation for doing the right thing, for doing what God would have wanted me to do.

When I shared the news with Chaplain Bob, Jamie, and my parents, they told me I did the right thing too. None of them wanted to tell me what I should do. I had to find out on my own. Although I lost the best job I had ever had at that time, I had taken a step in my life to listen to and obey the voice of God.

I found it difficult to trust people. After losing the job at the ISD I wondered if I would have to live my life looking over my shoulder, as if something unexpected would happen. I was broken and hurt inside. After all the years I had spent in prison I was still paying for the past. But I was not willing to give up. One of the things I learned after listening to Joyce Meyer was that God was not going to determine my future based on my past. I had a new life in Christ and He was going to sustain me and provide for my family. God had a plan and purpose for my life. My destiny was going to be achieved through Him.

Many times I told Lorie that if I had to live in a cardboard box out in the woods I would be happy with that. Sometimes she asked me details about prison life and most of the time I preferred not to talk about it. About the only thing I could talk about was the food I couldn't stand to eat anymore, except for ice cream. After Christ changed my life the experience of prison became a vivid reminder of how precious life is and how each and every moment is to be cherished. All of us tend to take things for granted as we rush through the business of life. We don't realize how every warm breeze and sunny sky is a gift from God. There is so much to be thankful for. I know that the times in my life when I have been the most thankful have been those times when I had very little. I make it a point to often thank God for everything regardless of how great or small because He places great value on every living creature. Nothing goes unnoticed by Him.

Chapter 14

One of the things I began to realize was that even though God had changed me and given me a new life, man did not look at me the way God did. Man always seemed to focus on the outside, while God looks at the heart. After I had lost the job I began to search for another job in my field. In Michigan several companies had been downsizing, and there was much competition for jobs in computer technology. If I got noticed because of my qualifications and had an interview, or an opportunity, I began to check to see if my background would be an issue. Sometimes the door would close immediately if they required a criminal background check. I began to wonder if I was doing what I was supposed to do. I had a passion for what I had been going to school for, and I was diligent in my studies and training. I had even prayed about it, asking the Lord if this was what I was supposed to be doing.

For several months I could not find work. During the winter months in our new home I often felt miserable and of little worth. My wife was working, and we were barely making the house payments. We continued to attend Resurrection Life Church in Grandville, which was now an hour drive one way. When we lived closer we were there more often. Now our trips were reduced to Sundays, and I began to feel like my relationship with the Lord was becoming distant as well. I felt rejected and angry. I decided to focus on my studies for school, and when not attending classes in the evenings I studied constantly during the day while Lorie was working.

During the winter months that I was searching for work I realize it was a testing period for me. The rejection and anger I felt was directed toward the world, not God. Many times I prayed and asked the Lord why this could happen. Before living for Christ my pattern in life was having an identity based on my career, but now my identity and purpose was living for the Lord. I had to learn to trust God and rely on Him regardless of the circumstances. This season of testing in my life was one of many that God used to make me stronger and teach me that regardless of what the world thought or did, God would never reject me.

In March I attended a men's conference at our church. Lorie and I had begun visiting some other churches close to home because of the driving distance, and it felt good to be back at our home church and to see some familiar faces. I ran into a good friend and brother in the Lord, Mark Sperlik. I had not seen Mark in some time, and I shared with him that Lorie and I had moved about an hour north of town. As we talked Mark told me about a sister church of our home church that had started about a year earlier, Resurrection Life Worship Center, and it was located about half the distance we were currently traveling, in Rockford, Michigan. He also introduced me to some men from the church that was there at the conference. One was the pastor of the men's ministry, a man named Keith Hemmila. We talked a bit, and Mark invited me to sit with them during the conference. We had a wonderful time, and they encouraged me to come and visit the church with my wife.

After the conference I told Lorie about seeing Mark, and about the new church in Rockford. We decided to visit on a Sunday in early spring and were pleasantly surprised to see so many familiar faces from our home church in Grandville. I was again greeted by Pastor Keith and other people we knew. We felt very welcome at the new church, and decided to visit a few times to see if this might be a place where we felt God calling us. Within a couple of months we decided to call it our new church home.

My pursuit of my degree was nearing an end. I had excelled at college. I poured myself into it, and by June I was ready to graduate with a bachelor's degree in Network Engineering. I had also been devoted to taking the technical examinations required for certifications and had passed many of them. The graduation ceremony for Davenport University had great significance for me. It had been just four and a half years before since I left the prison farm, and God had given me so much more than I had ever expected or dreamed possible. I had applied myself so diligently over the past few years, and I made the Dean's List every term that I attended. I like to joke that it was so much better to make the Dean's List instead of the Wanted List. I graduated with High Honors, but for me the honor and glory went to God, for without Him I could have never done it. And if not for the love, patience, and support of a loving wife it would have been a great struggle. Lorie sacrificed so much of our early marriage for me to pursue my education.

Now as I entered into graduation I felt like a young man again, even though I was 46 years old. Many of my family were there, including my mother, other immediate family members, and my beautiful wife Lorie. She had been, and still is my biggest fan. I called her that because she always cheered me on to complete whatever had been set before me. What a proud and joyful day it was for me to walk the isle that day. I could only say, *"Thank you Lord."*

That month of June in 2003 Lorie had found a full-time job closer to home, and I had found seasonal full-time work at the corporation I had worked for a year earlier. I was working with a group of young college kids selling tax forms and software to previous and existing customers for the upcoming year. I had been sending my resume out to different companies, but did not have any prospects until I got a call in late June.

A company in Grand Rapids that provided onsite computer technology services for several businesses contacted me. The owner had seen my resume posted at Davenport University and expressed an interest to talk to me. Mike Sr. had started this company almost 20 years earlier, and had raised four sons who were also involved in different aspects of the business.

The day of my interview he sent me into his office ahead of him and I noticed a book on his desk, *The Purpose Driven Life* by Rick Warren. I had read the book, and for a brief moment I thought this was a divine appointment. When Mike Sr. came into the office I mentioned the book to him, and we began to share. I found out that he had been a part of my old church in Grandville years earlier when it was just starting up, and he knew the pastor and several other people I had known for some time.

After I left the initial interview I was excited that I had been called to this business. I had never applied. They called me, so I believed in my heart that this had to be from God. I shared the news with Lorie when I got home, and she was also excited for me.

Within the next two weeks I had two more interviews for the job before they offered to hire me. I was hired as a Sr. Systems Analyst. My primary job responsibility was to provide onsite support for one of the local school districts. It covered five different schools, from elementary to high school, monitoring all their computer systems, providing technical support, and network administration. By July I had my hands full learning all the new systems.

It seemed that this was a year that brought other divine appointments in my life as well. Once in awhile I would stop at my Brother Ben's auto repair shop to have him do some repairs on one of our automobiles. I stopped by after work one day and saw my father, Ben Sr., standing there in the shop. He stepped outside and I followed him out. It had been over ten years since I had seen my dad. As I approached him I smiled and said *"Hi Dad."* He looked at me, almost not recognizing me, and I grabbed his hand, then put my arm around him and gave him a hug. He didn't know how to handle it, or what to say. I realized in that moment that I still loved him, and that I had never stopped. There was still a little boy in me that longed for the approval of his dad. All those years a part of me had hated him, until now.

I understood why my father did not recognize me that day. He saw Christ living in me, and I was changed. I had been transformed into someone he did not recognize. I began to tell my father about Christ, and how I had given my life to Him over ten years before. I told him how Jesus had changed my life, and that I no longer lived like I once did. While we were talking my wife Lorie pulled up in her car and I introduced my father to her. He was almost speechless. I don't think my father recognized me as the son he could control and manipulate at one time in my life. Before I left with Lorie that day I gave him another hug, and I told him I loved him.

That July I also got to know my new friends in men's ministry. Some of the leaders had organized a men's campout for the weekend. Everyone headed to a county campground located on a small lake where we rented adjoining sites for campers and tents. About a dozen men came, including Pastor Keith. I barely knew any of the men at that time. They knew little of me, except that I was a fellow brother in the Lord.

Friday evening we gathered around the campfire to talk and get acquainted. It was a good time to share and enjoy the time together. I had been longing for fellowship with other men for some time. This was my first opportunity in awhile to begin some new relationships since we had begun attending the new church. Most of the men were unfamiliar to me. Some I had seen at church since we began visiting, but I didn't know their names yet. I felt comfortable, but was reserved about talking about myself.

The next morning a few of us went out in a small fishing boat to spend some time fishing. It was a chilly morning and the fish were not biting. Nonetheless I was enjoying the peace and the beautiful portrait the Lord had painted that morning of the clear water and the wooded shoreline.

By mid-morning we had gone back to shore and joined the rest of the men. Some of the men had been playing horseshoes and riding bike, and around lunchtime everyone was back at camp preparing to grill some food. Various conversations were going on, and I overheard a couple of the men talking to Charlie, one of the men in our group. Something about him seemed familiar, but I couldn't figure it out. One of them spoke to Charlie something about prison ministry. I didn't catch the rest of the conversation, but when they had finished talking I started a conversation with Charlie and found out that he was a retired police officer. I told him I was a former state trooper from years ago, and asked him about his working in prison ministry, and in what capacity. As Charlie spoke his voice became more familiar to me, and when he told me that he had been going into Muskegon Correctional Facility for several years the pieces suddenly all fit together. This was Charlie Myers, the Grand Rapids police officer who had come into MCF to minister to prisoners, and I was one of those men. It had been almost eight years since I had seen Charlie, and I had never been this close to him. He had never met me personally when coming to the prison, and after all these years God had brought us together for this meeting. I mentioned to Charlie that I knew of the prison in Muskegon, and said to him, *"I remember you."* Charlie looked at me puzzled and asked if I was there. I said yes, and then even more puzzled he asked, *"Were you staff?"* I smiled at him again and said no. When I did that he realized that I had been in the prison as an inmate. Then I proceeded to tell Charlie my testimony about my past from police officer to convicted criminal, and how Christ had changed my heart, and my life. Charlie gave me a big hug, and tears welled up in my eyes with gratitude for how God had set this meeting to take place. It was an opportunity for me to thank Charlie for planting a seed in my life inside that prison those years before.

The rest of the day Charlie and I talked at length about our lives and various men we both knew who were serving God and still in prison. Here was a man who had dedicated 25 years of his life to law enforcement, and God had given him a desire to reach out to men behind bars. Charlie was still a big man with an even bigger heart.

Late in the day many of the men had met back at camp. Some were still out fishing. Those of us back at camp sat in a circle and began to share about different things God was doing in our lives. I had not planned to talk about myself or my past, but somehow I felt prompted by the Holy Spirit, and I began to tell the men about knowing Charlie from years before. I went into detail about my past as a police officer and the self-destruction that followed until I ended up in jail and prison. I talked about receiving Christ as my Lord and Savior, and all the profound changes God had made in my life, and how he had brought me to this place at this time in my life.

Some of the other men began to open up as well. One of the men had been dealing with alcoholism for years, and God was working on him to bring healing into his marriage and his life. On the outside none of us would have recognized what was going on within each of us. Something was happening here on this campout. New relationships were beginning. Barriers were breaking down, and God was moving in our midst.

(Men's ministry camp...From left Gary, Pastor Keith, Rick, Charlie Myers, & John)

I was getting to know Pastor Keith too. Here was a man who was passionate about the Lord and men's ministry. He had a vision for the things he desired to see happen. His desire was to see men become spiritual leaders in their homes and church, and for men to be real. It wasn't just character he was after. It was integrity built on relationships that stressed accountability. As I grew to know him I came to appreciate his strength and wisdom. He was not afraid to share with us the pain and hardship he had experienced in his life years before like many of us. I came to respect him even more.

After the weekend campout Pastor Keith and Charlie approached me to consider giving my testimony at a men's ministry gathering sometime in the future. They recognized something in me that I had not. Somehow God was going to use the testimony He had given me. I thought at first that I would consider it, and yet there was a part of me that was guarded because I was worried that someone might use my past to hurt me.

Men's ministry became very important to me. The relationships that I was developing with these men were more than friendships. They were becoming my brothers in Christ. I looked forward to our monthly meetings. Slowly bonds were forming, and growing stronger. I longed for spending more time with other Christian men. It had been over five years since I had enjoyed close relationships with men who were brothers in Christ while in prison. Now God had brought many new men into my life that I got to know and fellowship with. I was especially thankful for Charlie Myers and Pastor Keith. Charlie had witnessed firsthand the changes that God had made in my life, and along with Keith he recognized something in me that I could not see.

Lorie and I were together becoming more involved with our new church as well. When we joined Resurrection Life Worship Center in Rockford we developed many new relationships with other married couples from church, including the associate pastor, Larry Young and his wife Audrey. They taught the Married for Life classes at their home which Lorie and I attended for several weeks with about five other couples. The classes were very in-depth and it gave us a chance to get to know everyone much better. We were especially pleased for these new relationships because these people became as family to us. We liked to take advantage of marriage seminars and meetings to strengthen our marriage when opportunities came about. When Pastor Larry and his wife Audrey hosted the classes in their home it was a chance for us to fine tune our marriage and a great opportunity to get to know some of the other married couples in our church. Lorie and I were challenged in several areas of our marriage that helped us learn how to communicate better and have a greater understanding of each others needs.

We also started singing with the praise and worship team of the church, and felt blessed to be a part of this. We both loved to sing, and I had come to appreciate singing praises to God more than ever. There is nothing better than to come into the presence of God singing praises to him. Worship is something I became very passionate about. It wasn't just the singing, but experiencing the presence of Almighty God in our midst. Our lives felt full in many ways. I was pleased that we could serve God in this way.

The new job that I had started that summer for the Christian businessman Mike Sr. was going well. I poured myself into it. His son Mike Jr. was my Account Manager. He was probably one of the most technologically gifted men I had ever met. As an engineer he taught me many things. Mike Jr. also was a programmer, and many days I noticed the circles under his eyes from lack of sleep as he tried to catch up on work. The plan for him was to groom me to eventually take over management of the school districts and free him for other responsibilities.

As I got to know Mike Jr. better I developed great respect for him. He was also a Christian, and there were times when we got to talk about the Lord. It felt good to be in a workplace where I could talk about Christ. It seemed like I was walking in the plan that God had established before me. I appreciated Mike Jr. for the things he was teaching me, and the character he displayed. I could see that he was a man of integrity.

Chapter 15

By October Pastor Keith asked me if I would speak to a gathering for our monthly men's meeting and give my testimony. I had done this publicly in the past, just not in my local community or in my church. Previously I had given my testimony for Forgotten Man Ministries in Traverse City, Michigan and in Grand Rapids. The ministry began in 1961 with chaplains and volunteers who give their time to men and women in jails for the gospel of Christ. Chaplain Bob in Traverse City is part of the ministry, and he had asked me a couple of years before to give my testimony at an annual banquet. I was able to speak to a group of about 500 people that included local volunteers, officers in law enforcement, judges, chaplains, and people who provide financial support for the ministry. It was a joy in my life to share how Forgotten Man was used by God to touch my life. I had the opportunity afterwards to shake hands with the Sheriff's of the area, and one of the local judges who approached me afterwards. He had been one of my attorneys years ago, and now he was a judge. It was a moment in my life, like many, when God would touch my heart by reuniting me with someone from the past. I celebrate those moments when God's goodness shines.

I had also been asked by the chaplain of Forgotten Man in Grand Rapids to speak at their banquet a year earlier. Before the banquet started I was seated at one of the front tables with my wife Lorie. The Kent County Sheriff, Larry Stelma, was seated next to us and we began to talk. He knew I was speaking after the meal, and I began to talk to him about being a former state trooper. As I told him about the trouble I had many years before in the 1980's he said he remembered a former state trooper who had been arrested in his county during a break-in at a grocery store. He was the officer in charge that night at the scene of the scuffle and arrest. At that moment we both realized that it was the same night in March 1987 and that I was the arrested burglar. God had brought us together after all these years at this time and place. As we shook hands and talked about the Lord I realized that there is nothing more powerful than God's grace. No one could ever have imagined a dramatic change in a person's life unless they knew Christ. I was so thankful that God had reunited us that evening at the banquet.

I had also been going into the Traverse City jail for Christmas each year to speak to all the men and women, to tell my story as a fallen police officer, and of the years I spent in prison while Christ transformed the person I had been into someone new. Chaplain Bob had asked me to do this for their Christmas program, and it has since become an annual privilege that I look forward to. The main reason I believe the men and women listen is because I have credentials. What I mean by that is they can relate to me because I sat where they sat, wearing jail greens, incarcerated for crimes, and I spent many years in prison. My prayer each year is that God will touch at least one heart. So many times God has taken one person to impact thousands of lives.

My past was not common knowledge, and only a handful of men from my church had known about it. Now I had an opportunity to speak to several men in my own community for the first time. There were about 30 men present, including Charlie Meyer. God began to show me that He was going to use my testimony to touch people who were not involved in jail and prison ministry. I believe that God was bringing me to a new level in spiritual maturity and He was going to use me to do greater things for Him. As I gave my testimony I talked about my father and his background, his family, and his imprisonment. I spoke about never wanting to be like him since I was a young boy, how the pain I had carried all those years drove me to be an over-achiever until I met failure, and the pain I carried became anger. *Exodus 20:5-6 says "I, the LORD your God, am a jealous God, visiting the iniquity of the fathers on the children, on the third and the fourth generations of those who hate Me, but showing lovingkindness to thousands [of generations], to those who love Me and keep My commandments."* I had been in rebellion all of my life against God and in the end, because I did not serve God and love him the sins of my father became my own. I became the essence of what my father had represented.

All of my life I had built walls up around me and often seemed unemotional in times of turmoil. Yet when I spoke about Christ, and how he had changed me I became passionate. God had been doing something in me since I invited him into my heart, and now he was doing something greater, giving me a passionate desire to serve Him and know Him on a more intimate level than ever before.

After I had spoken at our men's ministry meeting my personal relationships with several of the men grew. I had also taken the opportunity to develop deeper relationships through accountability. A couple of years before I began meeting with a friend at work named Ernie. He had a similar background and he had fought the same struggles that I had fought. We had become very close and developed a relationship of trust and confidence. I believe that God brought us together so that we could share our burdens, pray for one another, and become stronger in our walk and faith as Christians. Now in men's ministry I had developed a couple of other relationships with men for accountability purposes. I maintained my weekly meetings in person or by phone with Ernie (and still do to this day). These relationships were something I had never known with my own father.

I was also pleased that God allowed me to have a closer relationship with one of the men I had known in prison at Muskegon. David and I had initially become friends in prison when I played softball, which developed into true fellowship through Christ. He had been released from prison a year or so earlier and lived close to Lorie and me. It was a joy to have him at our home for dinner many times and to invite him to church with us on several occasions as well. He became like a brother to me and a best friend in many ways. David also came to several Men's Ministry meetings and was there the night I gave my testimony.

Occasionally I saw my father at my Brother Ben's auto repair shop since that day we initially met after all those years. I always greeted him and tried to have a conversation with him, but I could tell he felt uncomfortable, especially when I tried to talk to him about the Lord. When I told him I was praying for him he laughed at me. I sensed bitterness from him, like he resented that I would pray for him. His attitude seemed to be that I was wasting my time. I longed to have my father know the Lord and have Christ in his heart. I hoped and prayed so much that somehow God could reach him, and yet I began to think that his heart would always be hard and bitter, and that he would never change. Even so I let him know that I loved him and I still called him dad. Each time I talked to him and walked away I wondered afterward if I would ever see him again.

When I was younger my father would drop in and out of my life at different times after he and my mother divorced when I was eight years old. It wasn't until I was in my mid-teens that I saw him again. Most of my life he had never been around and yet I still longed to know him and be a part of his life. Even when I was old enough to drive I would take my car to visit him when he wasn't in prison. He lived with his second wife in Grand Rapids, along with four sons and a daughter they had together during their marriage. My father never showed an interest in the things I liked and I remember trying to take an interest in the things he cared about, like cars and motor-cycles. When he went back to prison during my later teen years I even drove to the prison to visit him and take him necessities like clothing and money. After that I rarely spent time with him when he was not in jail, and most of the time it was only when he wanted to borrow some money or ask a favor.

By spring of 2004 I had focused on the battles and struggles I fought in my mind. After seeing my father at different times I still felt like I wasn't worthy to receive his approval. It seemed as if an ongoing war was waging regarding the past and my present. I knew that God had changed me, and yet I would allow thoughts to come in that I still wasn't good enough to have freedom to live a life free of doubt and suspicion. I would allow negative thoughts to flood into my mind, and I wanted to have a peace that would settle in my mind and rest there permanently. God had already healed me from so much, and I didn't want to have these personal battles anymore. I wanted to win the war. I began to read a book by Joyce Meyer called *Battlefield of the Mind*. As I read I visualized many of the same trials and tragedies I had faced as a Christian. I began to understand that the battles I was fighting were with the devil. I had allowed him to setup strongholds in my mind and they were controlling me. I began to write scriptures on note cards to carry with me and memorize. I would look at them throughout the day, especially when I felt negative thoughts enter into my mind. I began to meditate on these scriptures to remind myself of what God had already spoken to me through his Word. One of those scriptures helped me in forgetting the past. *"Do not [earnestly] remember the former things; neither consider the things of old. Behold, I am doing a new thing. Now it springs forth; do you not perceive and know it and will you not give heed to it? I will even make a way in the wilderness and rivers in the desert." Isaiah 43:18-19*

"I'm not where I want to be, but thank God I'm not where I used to be!" I had heard that familiar phrase many times spoken by Joyce Meyer in her tapes and books. It became a constant reminder for me in my spiritual warfare against the devil. One thing I had learned in my walk with God was that as I got stronger for the Lord the enemy always came at me harder. His greatest weapon had been using my past, but I was learning to look ahead. God's love for me was never based on my past. I knew I never deserved forgiveness and a life of freedom, but it was a gift given to me by God through his son Jesus. How comforting it is to know that He doesn't look at who I was. He sees me as I can be.

For years I did not understand what character was. Many people can look good on the outside. I had done that for years when I was living for myself. On the inside a person can be a crumpled mess and still appear quite the opposite on the outside. Learning to walk and be a man of integrity is so different. If I existed like a glass house and everyone could see through me would I still appear to be the same man of character? Is the real person that lives on the inside the person we see on the outside? Would I be ashamed of the real person I was? These are questions I asked myself many times. It didn't matter anymore how the world saw me. What mattered most was how God saw me, and how he sees me today. He knows the desires of my heart, and how I long to be all that he envisions for me. God was preparing me.

By late summer I had not seen my father for a few months. I had heard from my sister and brother Ben that our father's health was deteriorating, and that he was not able to care for himself. He had been forgetting things and showing signs of Alzheimer's disease, which is a progressive brain disorder that gradually destroys a person's memory and ability to learn, reason, make judgments, communicate and carry out daily activities. As Alzheimer's progresses, individuals may also experience changes in personality and behavior, such as anxiety, suspiciousness or agitation, as well as delusions or hallucinations. The burden for any family to take care of my father was too great, and a decision had to be made to have him live in a nursing home. My brother Ben and my sister Micki had power of attorney to make the decision. Within a few months our father had been living in one nursing home and then another. He was unmanageable and unruly. He would curse those who tried to take care of him, including my younger brother Randy. He had always been there for our father, tending to his every need, and when Randy had to be the one to take our father to a different home he cursed Randy as he had done to his caregivers. His words tore Randy's heart, and afterwards my brother refused to see him again. It was a terrible wound that could not be healed. I had heard about the incident later on from my sister and all I could do was pray. What would it take for God to get my father's attention?

By August I had been at my job for 13 months. I had worked very hard to demonstrate leadership and the ability to adapt quickly. Technology is constantly changing, and I had proven that I was a dedicated employee. I had gained the confidence and trust of my project manager Mike Jr. We had many conversations about work, and he reminded me on more than one occasion that I would be taking a greater responsibility in the future. During the summer months he had given me the opportunity to take on projects and delegate team members to accomplish them. I was looking forward to the challenges that lay ahead.

Early one morning I had been one of the first persons to arrive at the office. I would customarily arrive at the office early to review issues at one of our customer sites, and then prioritize my schedule according to the most critical ones. Sometimes I would meet with Mike Jr. to discuss problems or projects that needed to be addressed. On this particular morning he asked to speak with me, and thinking nothing out of the ordinary I sat down next to him at his desk to talk. He pushed some papers over the top of the desk for me to examine, and he asked me the question, *"Is that you?"* As I looked down on the desk I recognized my criminal records. As I went through the pages the records indicated that the record was that of John Joseph Piper. I had been living under my legal name John Richard Collier for over six years since I left prison. Without hesitation I looked at Mike Jr. and said, *"Yes, that was me years ago. But that man doesn't exist anymore."* I reminded Mike of *2 Corinthians 5:17* which says, *"Therefore, if anyone is in Christ, he is a new creation; the old has gone, the new has come!"* He nodded in agreement with me, and said my job could be in jeopardy. He recognized that I was not required to provide any criminal background when I was hired for the job, and I had not misled the company. But the problem was that I was working in a school district, and he would have to go over the contract with them to see if there were any violations or issues with the contract.

In the meantime I returned to work as usual. I felt at peace about my conversation with Mike Jr. and I believed in my heart that I acted with good intentions. I believe God was pleased with me that day. I told my wife Lorie about it after work and we prayed about it, knowing that God would see us through whatever happened.

Mike Jr. did not tell me during our conversation, but I learned later that the information he received was provided by someone I had interviewed with for a job over a year earlier. I had provided the information during the course of an interview when I was questioned whether I had a criminal past. I answered truthfully, and the information was given with the assurance that it would be kept in strict confidence. The release of such information was a violation of the policy of the organization, and a breach of confidentiality. In layman's terms it was unethical. The person responsible may have thought they were doing a good deed when in fact they may have been liable for a lawsuit. My reaction to this was not anger or bitterness. In my heart I was hurt, but I did not react. It was for God to deal with that person.

For the next two weeks Mike Jr. fought for my job. On a Monday morning I showed up early at the office as usual. As I arrived I noticed that his father Mike Sr. was there, which was unusual. He was rarely there early, unless there was a scheduled meeting. Mike Jr. approached me to tell me that his father wanted to talk to me. I knew what was going to happen before I went into his office, and God's peace covered me. I felt at ease while Mike Sr. was obviously very uncomfortable. I found out that there was no breach of the contract with the school district, but to keep their contract in good standing I was about to become a sacrifice.

Mike Sr. told me he didn't have a choice, and something to the effect that *"I thought I knew you."* As he spoke those words I thought in my heart *if he believes God's Word then he would know me.* But such was not the case on this day. Here was a man I had respected. Perhaps he could have used me in the business sector of the company, but I was never given the opportunity. Instead he gave me the option to quit my job with a severance package that amounted to an additional two weeks pay. He wanted to wash his hands of me quickly and quietly. And if I didn't quit he was going to terminate me. When my criminal history came up during my conversation with Mike Sr. I believe that he expected some kind of reaction out of me, and when he didn't get one he was very surprised. The higher level of maturity that God brought me to enabled me to be strong and to know without doubting that the Lord was going to provide something even better for me.

I knew that if I resigned as he wished and walked out I would not have any compensation of any kind until I found a new job. I had to think of my wife and providing for her. I told him I would write a letter of agreement that would allow me to collect compensation until I found a new job, and that I would provide it within 48 hours. Then I gave my security codes and keys to Mike Jr., and I walked out.

When I went home early that day Lorie was there. She had a curious look on her face, and I shared the news about what happened. She recognized that I was not in distress, and I told her it was alright. God had provided for us in the past, and we agreed in prayer that He would continue to watch over us. It was not devastating as it had been almost two years earlier when I had worked for the intermediate school district.

I made several calls that day and contacted a couple of different attorneys. I spoke to one that specialized in unfair labor practices, and another that specialized in civil lawsuits. I didn't want to sue anyone. I didn't feel that was what God wanted me to do. I just wanted to be careful about how I was going to proceed, and I wanted to be sure that our finances would not become a burden. In the end I contacted Mike Sr. and told him I had spoken to a couple of different attorneys, and if he wanted to give me a layoff from work I would agree to that. I would not resign. He agreed, and I sent a letter to his office regarding the terms of my leaving.

Even in the midst of what had happened I knew God was present in my life looking over me. For the past two years I had been studying for certifications in my field and had been working hard to achieve the certification of Microsoft Certified Systems Engineer. I had completed and passed six of the seven required exams, and when I worked for Mike Sr. he encouraged me to complete my testing and pass the final test to achieve the goal I had been pursuing. I had already taken the test twice and failed. Two days after leaving the company I walked out of a testing facility after passing the final exam. It was bittersweet. As I sat in my car and praised God I wept. I had no idea what the future held for me. I was very confused.

Chapter 16

During the next two weeks I updated my resume and began to search for a job. I started looking for opportunities with ministries. Perhaps God could use me in a place where I would not be rejected and I would be embraced. I began to question if I was supposed to be in Michigan, or if I should look elsewhere. I started to seek God and pray about what He wanted for Lorie and me. I always knew the Lord had a plan and purpose for our lives. I had read the scripture many times in *Jeremiah 29: 11-13* which says, *"For I know the plans I have for you," declares the LORD, "plans to prosper you and not to harm you, plans to give you hope and a future. Then you will call upon me and come and pray to me, and I will listen to you. You will seek me and find me when you seek me with all your heart."*

I remember now in the days after leaving my job Lorie and I had been listening to a series of messages from Joyce Meyer and she had been talking about getting *double for your trouble.* It became a theme around the house for me. Somehow I felt the Holy Spirit speaking to my heart telling me that God was getting ready to bring a greater blessing to me.

One thing I learned is that God can turn a curse into a blessing. *(Deuteronomy 23:5) "But the LORD thy God turned the curse into a blessing unto thee, because the LORD thy God loved thee."* A blessing also starts with an utterance. It is to speak well of or to praise God. You can bless God by your life, by loving Him and obeying Him. When we praise God we are blessing Him; we speak blessings to God and to Jesus! Because blessings start with words, when we speak the blessings of God to a person in the name of Jesus Christ, those things are imparted into their lives. When we speak blessings into a person's life, these blessings have much more authority and power than do curses. In my daily prayers and devotions I began to speak blessings into our lives through the scriptures, and I would write them down on note cards to remind me of the plans God had for my life.

I had been content living where we were, but as I searched for work it seemed that there were no opportunities available to me. Lorie had also been researching. She mentioned to me that Joyce Meyer Ministries in Fenton, Missouri had a few job opportunities in technology that might be of interest to me. My initial response was that it was too far away. But as I thought about it I realized what an impact Joyce's ministry had made on my life, and how God had used her to touch our lives many times. Perhaps God would give me an opportunity to be a small part of a ministry that touches lives all over the world. Inside I felt somewhat insignificant after the rejection I had received so many times in the past, but in faith I sent an application with my resume to the ministry headquarters.

Two weeks later I received a phone call from a small computer technology company in Muskegon, Michigan, about sixty miles from my home. It was owned by a couple of local men, and one of them called me to see if I might be interested in an opportunity for a position with their company. There were no questions on the application or at the interview regarding criminal history, and less than a week after the interview I accepted a high paying position as a network engineer. I concluded that God had provided something better for me financially.

Within six weeks of starting the job I felt in my heart that it was not a good fit for me. I felt out of place, and it was very stressful and demanding. I worked very hard to adapt but could not. By Thanksgiving I met with one of the owners and agreed that the job was not working out for me. I was very disillusioned by then. As I drove home I was ready to give up searching for any job. I was beginning to wonder if there was any place in the world where God could use me.

I spent a lot of time in my prayer closet (so to speak) during the months that I sought God and His plans for my life. Emotionally I was feeling almost lost, as if I could do nothing without the Lord. I was totally reliant on Him like a lamb that is helpless without the shepherd to protect it. I needed God more than ever and I was ready for Him to take me by the hand to lead me down the path He had already established for me to follow.

My focus shifted from finding a job to concentrating on my relationship with the Lord. Perhaps God was trying to teach me something. I felt a deep need to know what His purpose was for my life. One of the things that Pastor Keith had encouraged me to consider was journaling. He had shared with me and the other men from the men's ministry about how it had impacted his life. I had been considering it for months, but kept putting it off. By the end of January in 2005 I finally purchased a journal and began to write.

Within a week I received a call from Joyce Meyer Ministries. It had been six months since I had applied for a position, and now they were calling to see if I was still interested in a job with the ministry. I also learned from one of the pastors at my church that someone from the ministry headquarters in Fenton had called him to ask several questions about me.

My first interview by telephone in February of 2005 lasted about an hour and a half. I later wrote in my journal how the peace of God covered the conversation, and how thankful I was for the simple opportunity to even be considered for a position working for Joyce Meyer. Regardless of the outcome I felt the Lord telling me that I mattered and that there was a place for me in the world.

For the next week we received unexpected prayers from several people. One of the ministries we had supported sent us a card in the mail to let us know that God had put it on their hearts to pray for us. I also received a call from Pastor Keith. He prayed for me as well, believing that God's perfect plan was unfolding in our lives. God was using the prayers and love of many people to cover us with His protection and to remind us of His presence.

In the following days to come I lived with expectancy and wrote in my journal daily. We had not received word yet from Joyce Meyer Ministries, but I prayed that Lorie and I would have a secure future with no more surprises. I believed God for a place where we would not be hurt again. I also praised God daily for His love and for the strength he gave us.

Two weeks after my telephone interview with Joyce Meyer Ministries I received a call from their Human Resources department inviting me to come to Missouri for a job interview. Lorie and I were very excited and at the same time a great peace covered us. I felt the Lord reminding me to maintain my inner peace and to live peaceably, with the confidence that He was in control of our lives and that His perfect plan was unfolding. I could feel God speaking, *"Be still and know that I am God." Psalm 46:10*

For several months since I had initially applied for the job with Joyce Meyer Ministries Lorie and I had agreed not to talk to anyone about it. We prayed about it and wanted to seek God's leading in this area of our lives. By the time we left for Missouri in late February we had a great expectancy. A week before leaving I had written in my journal, *"Today I wakeup remembering the thoughts (vision) for my life this year, that this will be the greatest year of my life...My heart overflows with joy, excitement, and anticipation for what God has in store for me and Lorie, and I will continue to be in awe of God as He reveals His plan. Thank you Lord for your love and mercy, for the plan you've had for my life all along."*

I was honored and humbled to have the opportunity to travel to Fenton, Missouri to interview for the position with Joyce Meyer Ministry. When Lorie and I made the trip we were very excited when we saw the ministry headquarters for the first time. My motivation was based solely on determining if this was where God wanted us to be. After the recent events in my life for the past year before going to Missouri I was ready to answer the calling of God without question.

At the interview in Fenton I met with three people, including Andrea deCento, the lady that had interviewed me by phone, Carol Piles, the head of human resources, and Eric, one of the engineers in charge of the information technology division. Before we began I told them I had felony convictions dating back to 1992. They asked about the nature of the offenses and I explained, giving a brief testimony of my life as a police officer turned criminal, and how I had received Christ as my Savior in jail that same year in 1992. They did not dwell on the past or drill me with questions, but understood how God transforms people. I did not feel confident during the interview regarding my experience in technology, but I believe they were more interested in my character as a Christian. I could almost hear the devil telling me *"You're not good enough."* But God spoke to me and reminded me that He would meet my needs with His hands, in His time, and in His way. I was to yield my will to His control and pray as Jesus did, *"Not my will, but yours be done." (Luke 22:42)* I had to allow God to fulfill his purpose and plan for my life.

I felt a great peace as we returned to Michigan. Even though my body and mind were tired my spirit was calm. I longed to hear God's voice and to see His face. I would wait and listen for Him to speak to me and direct my steps, living one day at a time, knowing that God was in control.

After returning home I began to read *Approval Addiction, Overcoming Your Need to Please Everyone* by Joyce Meyer. As I read about the need for approval and acceptance from others I saw myself in the pages. I understood the feelings of guilt and condemnation brought on by rejection. It had affected me in every area of my life, and no matter how much I achieved I still felt like I had to do more. I never received the approval of my father as a young boy, and as I grew older I sought approval from every person I could. It had affected every area of my life. Reading this book began a healing in me that I did not expect. Within a few short months God would move to bring about the greatest healing in my life I had ever received.

During the next month we had not heard anything from the ministry in Missouri. On March 17, I wrote in my journal, *"...I don't know what God's plans are for me. For the first time in my life I don't know what I am going to do. I ask God to show me, to speak to my heart, to give me a passion for something that will change my life, something that will give me a purpose and support my family. Please Lord, direct me, show me where to go, what you would have me do. Who am I, and what am I here for? To serve you and to live each day for you. All my hope is in you."*

At the church we had been attending for the last two years Lorie and I both sensed emptiness. Something was missing. We had been serving in ministry but many things had changed. I was the first to say something to Lorie. In my heart I felt God calling us to go else-where. There seemed to be a lot of changes going on around us and no one, including the pastor, said anything to us with an explanation. We had been faithful servants and given our all. Yet somehow we sensed that this was no longer our home, and that God was calling us to move on. This had never been a practice for us in the past to leave our church family based on a feeling, but in my heart I knew that I was no longer growing in the Lord. Even though leaving was difficult it turned out to be a wise decision.

Pastor Keith and his wife Judy had been called by God to begin a new ministry and in the first month of April we went to visit on a Sunday evening. As we worshipped in the presence of God that night I felt brokenness in my heart, a deep longing for God. I had waited on the Lord and He had drawn me to this place where He wanted me to be. It was a small gathering of less than 30 people, but the overpowering presence of the Holy Spirit covered everyone.

It was here that God began to re-establish in me the purpose for my life through Jesus Christ. God spoke into my life to show me that the destiny He had established for my life would come when I had pursued God with all of my heart. That time in my life was about to arrive through Cleansing Stream.

The Cleansing Stream was introduced to us by Pastor Keith and his wife Judy. The mission *"is committed to partnering with pastors and churches in teaching and training leaders and maturing believers in personal cleansing, deliverance, and spiritual warfare so they can be released to serve, minister, and disciple others in the Body of Christ."* The best way I can describe the ministry is that it helps mature Christians get the junk out of their lives. Many Christians carry scars, soul ties, and bondages from their past that need to be broken. This ministry is one of deliverance that brings healing and freedom. Written by Dr. Jack Hayford, Founding Pastor of The Church on the Way in Van Nuys, California, the ministry partners with pastors and churches to develop mature Christians to guide and teach the principles of the Cleansing Stream.

We learned more about the ministry by leaders from Mount Hope Church in Lansing, Michigan who visited us on a Sunday evening in late March. All of these people were mature believers that had gone through the Cleansing Stream teachings for 10-16 weeks, which culminates in a regional weekend retreat where believers from several churches gather for teaching, worship, prayer, and deliverance. The testimonies of these people who came to visit us were incredible stories of victories and healings that encouraged us to begin attending the classes.

I was still unemployed as Lorie and I began to attend the weekly teaching, but it gave me an opportunity to study the materials in the workbook I received and to focus on the reading that included walking in the spirit, committing everything to God, and speaking words of life.

After several weeks had passed and the time was nearing to attend the weekend retreat I did not know if Lorie and I would be able to go. Our finances were strained with me not working and it was a burden for us to attend. Pastor Tim, the Associate Pastor asked me if we would be going, and then I explained that I doubted we could afford the hotel and the retreat. He informed me that a scholarship fund had been established for people who did not have the funds and encouraged me to go. I was grateful to accept the generosity of someone who had provided the opportunity for Lorie and me to go.

I felt urgency from God to attend this event. As we fasted and prayed during the week before making the trip to the retreat I did not know what to expect. In my spirit I had felt that I was at a turning point in my life, following down a path where God was leading me to a destiny I had not yet fulfilled.

The weekend retreat was being held at Mount Hope Church in Lansing. We arrived at the hotel at around 5:00 pm to check in and prepared to meet at the church with the rest of our group when the event was scheduled to begin at 7:00. As we arrived and entered the foyer of the church we were greeted by people at the door and directed to tables outside the sanctuary where we registered and picked up our name badges. People were lined up outside the doors. Promptly at 7:00 the doors opened and as we entered we were greeted by two long lines of volunteers on each side of us. There must have been about 60-70 people wearing designated colors for the specific functions they would serve during the weekend. As we entered we were greeted as if we were part of a celebration. Everyone was shaking our hands, welcoming us into this place. The worship team of musicians and singers were leading in praise and worship already. As we filed into our seats we felt great joy to join in on what seemed like the beginning of something awesome. I sensed a great expectancy among all the people.

As the praise and worship stopped we were introduced to one of the leaders of the retreat. There were approximately 700 people in the sanctuary, and at the front one of the leaders explained the format of the retreat. We would cover teaching in several different areas that stemmed from the lessons we studied and from the classes we had already attended. Each area covered specific areas where people needed healing in their lives. After each session of teaching everyone in the sanctuary would come up to the front to receive prayer, regardless of whether we personally believed we needed prayer in that area or not. Many people carried scars and needed healing in areas of their lives that they might not even realize.

At the front of the sanctuary was a red line marked across the floor that represented the blood of Christ. As each person crossed the blood line volunteers were lined up at the alter to pray for each individual. The volunteers had specific functions that included anointed prayer people, helpers, and others. As people in the lines crossed over the blood line and went forward for prayer an anointed prayer person laid hands on that person and prayed over them. The praise and worship began during this time as well, and as we waited in line we quietly prayed for God to prepare each of us individually and to reveal to our hearts any areas that needed healing. Then after prayer we returned to our seats to praise and worship in singing until everyone in the sanctuary had been prayed over.

One of the areas they taught on that first night was fear of rejection. In the weeks prior to coming to the retreat I finished reading the book *Approval Addiction* by Joyce Meyer. I remembered seeing myself in the pages of the book and I recognized the pattern of addiction I had lived trying to gain the approval of everyone I knew. As I crossed the bloodline that night I stood in front of an anointed woman named Angel. She didn't know me. She had never met me and did not know anything about me. That night she was indeed an angel to me because God spoke through her to me. Angel began to pray over me and speak to me about my father. I was still carrying within myself painful scars from my father and I didn't know it. Even though I had forgiven my father from the past I had buried the pain deep inside me. It was the spirit of rejection. I didn't realize it but there was actually a part of me that was rejecting God because I was afraid of being rejected by Him. I had not trusted God 100%. The walls that I had built up since my childhood were still around me. As God began to speak I heard His voice saying the words from *Isaiah 41:9, "I have chosen you and not rejected you."* God continued to speak through Angel with these words, *I'll never reject you. You don't need to fear. You don't need to gain anyone's approval. I am your Father.* Those words broke me inside as God revealed to me a picture of my past life that suddenly became clear, and I broke down weeping uncontrollably. I was still carrying all these wounds from my father and I never fully understood until that moment. Then the walls that had surrounded me all those years were immediately torn down. It was as if God had taken a giant sledge hammer and crumbled it and freed me from the prison I had built within myself. All the pictures of my life suddenly flooded in and I remembered when I sat in a prison cell. It was in that moment I realized that the person I hated most I had become. All my life I had hated my father, never wanting to be like him, and in the end I became him. At a time in my life before Christ became my Savior I was destined to die. My life was once spiraling straight down. I had no idea that God had a plan and purpose for me, and that Christ would change my life. Now He brought me healing and freedom greater than I had ever known. I no longer had to carry this pain from my past.

God's timing is always perfect. I never knew what He had in store for me when Lorie and I began to attend Crossfire Ministry and get involved in the Cleansing Stream. If we had not left our previous church when we did I don't believe that all the events that unfolded in our lives would have occurred precisely as they did. It could only happen with God using all these things to work together. Romans 8:28 says, *"And we know that all things work together for good to them that love God, to them who are the called according to his purpose."* I had traveled beyond the crossroads in my life to receive a healing from God with my father that I previously thought was impossible. It was beyond what I could ever imagine.

After the retreat I was so happy to share my testimony with our new church family and others that had been healed at Cleansing Stream. I had seen and heard of many miraculous healings that weekend. In the days and weeks to come I had no idea what God had in store for me. It's amazing what happened because suddenly I had boldness to go and see my natural father. My whole life I had never been able to tell my father what I really felt because I was always afraid of him rejecting me.

I had not seen my father for just over a year now. It was early May of 2005 and I had learned from my sister where he was. Since he had been diagnosed with Alzheimer's disease I was told that he was in the early stages of dementia. His mind was slowly becoming confused about places, dates, and people. God spoke to my heart and told me that I needed to go and see my father.

After I arrived at the nursing home that day I prayed in my car, asking God to give my father recognition to know who I was, and to give him the ability to understand what I was about to share with him. After I stopped at the desk and found out his room number I walked down the hallway and found the room with his name on the door. As I entered the room I saw him sitting in a recliner. He was dressed in a shirt and jeans and held a cane next to him. I remained silent to see if he would recognize me. He looked at me and called me by name, and told me he had been thinking of me. I said, *"I've been thinking about you too Dad."* I approached my father and he held out his hand to shake mine. I grabbed it and then put my arms around him and held him tightly. As I sat down I proceeded to tell my father *"Dad the reason I'm here is because God sent me to see you, and He told me you're going to die. If I die today I know where I'm going, and if you were to die today I want you to know where you are going too."* I talked to my dad about Jesus, and for the first time in my life I prayed with him. We prayed together the prayer of salvation, and as I held my dad we both wept.

I walked out of the nursing home that day knowing that my dad was right with God. He could no longer act phony as he had in years past, and even though his mind was almost like that of a child I knew he understood, and that for the first time in my life I could have a relationship with my father based on Christ. I no longer needed my father's approval. Now God was using me to teach my dad about Jesus, and how much the Lord loves him too.

In the weeks that followed the Cleansing Stream retreat I began to experience with my father the ability to share my feelings and emotions more than I ever had before, and my father was doing the same with me. As a young boy and even during the later years of my life it was difficult to truly express these things to my father because of the fear I had of being rejected. I'm sure that it was a pattern established by my father because he was never able to show me his real feelings and emotions until now. I'm sure that when he had lived most of his life selfishly with a hardened heart it would have made him feel vulnerable to truly express himself. But now my father was free. We both were. God was shining His bright light through us and allowing us to express the love of a father and son that we had never experienced before.

I continued to go and see my father every week, always praying and asking God to give him the ability to know me and understand what I was going to share with him. I paused on each visit as I walked in the door for my father to call me by name. I began to teach him about the life of our Savior Jesus and read the Bible to him. The first time I read to my father I read to him from John Chapter 14 where Jesus talked to the disciples and said, *"I am going there to prepare a place for you. And if I go and prepare a place for you, I will come back and take you to be with me that you also may be where I am. You know the way to the place where I am going."* I explained to my father that Jesus was talking to him too with those words, and that He had prepared a place for him in heaven already.

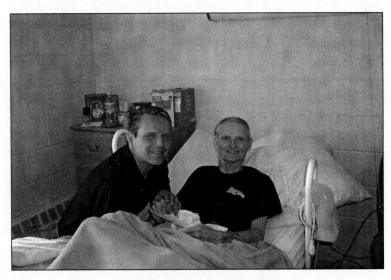

(John and his father Ben)

My greatest joy with my father was on the days I went to visit him at the nursing home. His eyes always grew brighter when I came into the room and I greeted him with a hug and a kiss. Sometimes when I walked into his room he was asleep and I stood next to his bed for awhile to watch him while he peacefully rested. I often gazed at him for a long time and quietly thanked the Lord for all He had done to make this precious time with my father possible. When I gently touched his hands his eyes would open, his countenance became brighter, and a smile widened across his face.

Each day that I read the Bible to my father his gaze upon me became more intent. I would read the scriptures to him, and then pause to explain the meaning of what God was saying through His Word. During those moments my father thanked me and expressed how much he appreciated me reading and praying with him. God's Word had come to life for my father as it had done for me. I could not ask for a greater gift from God.

I also began to teach my father how to pray, and we prayed the Lord's Prayer together. Each time my father and I did something like this for the first time I could feel the arms of God around us, holding us tightly, providing comfort and love that I had never experienced with my father until now. Many of these days my eyes filled with tears of joy to see God touching my dad.

My dad also had never heard me sing all of my life, and I remember the day I sat in his room with him and sang to him for the first time. It was a song of praise to God, and my dad stared intently at me with his deep blue eyes and held onto my hand. When I finished he told me how he loved it when I did that, as if I had been doing it all along. I am forever thankful to God for that precious moment with my father.

I'm so thankful that God doesn't determine my future based on my past. I could never imagine the depth of His love for me or the grace he gives me each day until knowing Jesus Christ as my Lord and Savior. When His plan for my life unfolds and I realize God's perfect timing I am awed. God always had a plan for my father's life as well. I was ready to give up on my father but the Lord never did. God never gives up on anyone. When all seemed lost for me there was still hope because Jesus paid the penalty for every sin I had committed, and He paid the penalty of death for my father as well.

Chapter 17

Within a month after I had first gone to see my father I started a new job. I applied for a job as a network administrator with an insurance company in Grand Rapids. I had read about the opportunity in the Sunday newspaper and sent a letter with my resume the following day. The job application asked for criminal convictions within the last seven years. It had been 13 years since I had been convicted of a felony, so I wasn't required to provide any history of my past. After two interviews I was offered a position and started work the following week in late May.

After my first week on the job Joyce Meyer Ministries called my wife Lorie. She had also applied for a job with the ministry earlier in the year. Our prayer was that if God called us to the ministry in Missouri we would both have jobs. Now they had called Lorie for a phone interview and she was very excited.

Our hearts were also becoming attached to Crossfire Ministries where Pastor Keith Hemmila and his wife Judy Buffum-Hemmila had begun a new church. As Lorie and I continued to attend the church the relationships with our new church family became very precious to us. Keith and Judy took special care to shepherd us as we followed the journey of Cleansing Stream. After the great healing that had taken place with my father they were especially excited after seeing what God had done in my life, and now that we were a part of their church we felt it was where God wanted us to be.

On one particular Saturday I had lunch with Keith and Judy after helping them move some furniture into the new church office. We were excited to talk about all the healings that occurred at Cleansing Stream, but God had been tugging on my heart to share something else with Judy. Over ten years earlier she was the woman who had come into a prison with Charlie Myers to minister to me and hundreds of other men in Muskegon, Michigan. She had never heard my testimony about prison, so she did not know that I was a man that she once ministered to. After lunch Keith began to talk to some people he knew in the restaurant and I took the opportunity to thank Judy personally and tell her that I was one of those men she ministered to years ago. She had planted a seed in my life like so many, and God used that seed to help me grow into the man I had become. Now once again after all these years God used Judy and her husband Keith to touch my life by introducing me to the Cleansing Stream Ministry and also inviting Lorie and me to become a part of the Crossfire Ministries family. The relationship that Lorie and I developed with Pastor Keith and Judy became very precious to us. It was especially valuable for me to share with Judy how much she had touched my life those years earlier. The day that we spoke in the restaurant we both wept as I told her how God had used her in my life. Since that time both she and Keith have been as dear family to us and we love them. Both of them truly demonstrate Christ with the love they show for others, and the kindness of their hearts. They have been as shepherds for many of us, protecting us from the enemy, and treating each of us as precious gems.

After Lorie's telephone interview with Joyce Meyer Ministries in late May we did not hear any news for some time. In the weeks that followed I felt quite comfortable with my new position and enjoyed it very much. God had given me a new peace, and my job was very challenging and rewarding. I constantly received reports of praise and appreciation from the employees, including management, and I was beginning to feel that perhaps this was the place that God had prepared for me to have a future. My daily devotions were spent praising the Lord for all He had done in our lives, and for the healing God had provided with my father. I continued to visit with him each week, reading God's Word to him, and praying with him.

I had something I never experienced with my Dad before, and I was in awe of how God blessed our time together.

Then during the second week of July something totally unexpected happened. I received a phone call from Joyce Meyer Ministries in Fenton, Missouri. I had not talked to them since my interview in late February, and now the human resources manager, Carol Piles was calling to see if I was still interested in a job with the ministry. At first I was totally dumbfounded and confused. They had interviewed my wife Lorie by phone in late May, but had not talked to me for months. I had understood that the ministry always prays over all their job applicants, but after not hearing from them in five months I thought that the job had been offered to someone else.

I was not sure what to say, so I asked Carol if I could talk to my wife and contact her later in the week. For the rest of the week Lorie and I prayed and sought God, asking Him to speak to our hearts. By Friday we were not yet sure and I contacted Carol in Fenton to ask for another week before making a decision. She understood the importance of a decision of this magnitude and gave us the time we had asked for.

I also spent much time in prayer asking God why I received a call now after I had a wonderful job and a new relationship with my father that I never had before. Then God reminded me of the events that had taken place in my life in the months since February with Cleansing Stream and the healing that He brought into my life. God was preparing me. Now as the Lord spoke to my heart I realized He had done so much for me, and now it was time for me to make whatever sacrifice necessary to serve Him.

God always confirmed things for me by His Word and through others. I had been reading about Abraham in *Genesis Chapter 12.* God had spoken to him and told him to leave his country, his father's household, his land and his goods, and to *"go to the land I will show you" (vs.1)* I felt God speaking those words to my heart and I shared it with Lorie as we prayed for God's will in our lives.

That same week we also watched Joyce Meyer on television and she talked about taking the next step, not being afraid to do what it takes to go into the Promised Land, that place God has prepared for us. As I listened to Joyce speak it gave me confirmation that we were being called by God. We were on a journey to do great things for Him. Ten years earlier I could never imagine the future that God had planned for us. I realized that my life belonged to Him, and that now it was my turn to give all I could for Jesus.

Lorie expressed concern about selling our home, moving away from family and friends, and the church we had become a part of. But she agreed with me that this was what God had asked of us and on Friday July 15th I made the call to Fenton and accepted the job with Joyce Meyer Ministries. We were given plenty of time to prepare and I was scheduled to begin my new job the day after Labor Day.

One thing I've learned is that as soon as God starts doing big things in our lives the devil begins to attack. On the same day that I accepted the new job my step-daughter Jessica, who is Lorie's youngest daughter, had a series of seizures and was rushed to the hospital by ambulance. When Jessica suffered a seizure that night in July Lorie rushed to the hospital with her older sister Diane. We learned later that Jessica had been dehydrated and had not eaten all day. Even though Jessica recovered in the following days Lorie always stayed in close contact to monitor her progress. Then within a week Lorie had two minor car accidents. The enemy used these incidents to try to bring fear into our home, but I remained steady and followed the course I believed God had been directing.

We had not shared the news about Joyce Meyer Ministries with anyone. We had waited on God to speak in our lives and now it was time to ask for the prayers and support of others. We contacted our pastor and his wife and shared the news with them. We asked them to pray for us as we prepared to make the move to Missouri. We were not ready to let everyone else know yet as we still needed to talk to our immediate families. When we shared the news with Pastor Keith and Judy about going to Fenton, Missouri to work for Joyce Meyer Ministries they were very excited and supportive of us. We depended on them even more for guidance. This was a new journey we were about to take in our lives and we needed the advice of someone we could trust. They were there to love and support us with their prayers and wisdom.

I also had to make a decision about informing my present employer. I had been with them for two months and now I was going to have to give them notice that I was leaving soon. It was very difficult determining exactly when the right time would be. I wanted to give them adequate notice, but I wanted to wait until at least two to three weeks before we moved to Missouri. I was afraid that they would be disgruntled about me leaving and dismiss me early before I was scheduled to leave.

Within two weeks after I accepted the new job Joyce Meyer Ministries called Lorie and scheduled a job interview with her in Missouri. This was just more confirmation for me that we were following the course that God had laid out for us. As we prepared to drive to Fenton for a weekend I had arranged to take the following Monday off so I could go with Lorie. But as the day approached for us to leave Lorie became more and more uneasy. I felt that she was giving in to fear because of the recent events and I reminded her that fear comes from the enemy and not from God. By the time we drove to Missouri that weekend in early August Lorie had become almost rebellious in her attitude about making the trip. On the drive down we didn't talk, and by the time I had driven over halfway there she mentioned that the trip was a waste of time and that she didn't know why we were going. She was having a battle with her emotions and I was trying to maintain control. I must have prayed the entire eight hours on the road.

The trip back to Fenton for Lorie's interview was a reality check. I think that when we made the trip earlier in February it seemed like a grand adventure of what could be. Now that we were going back it was no longer just an adventure. It was the real thing. I think that when it began to sink in with Lorie is when she got uncomfortable. I had taken the attitude that I was determined to follow the calling of God no matter what the cost. I was ready to take the next step. Lorie on the other hand began to feel apprehension and anxiety. My impression at the time was that the enemy was trying to bring fear into our midst and I was not going to put up with it.

We arrived in Fenton on a Saturday and checked in to a local hotel. After unpacking we drove over to the ministry headquarters to check time and driving distance. We also drove around to explore the city and look at apartments. On our previous trip in February we had taken the opportunity to check out some possible places to live so we were somewhat familiar with where we thought we might like to settle. After not talking most of the way down Lorie was talking to me now and I thought she was loosening up and more accepting of our new future.

By Sunday morning Lorie was struggling again emotionally. I went out for a morning jog and called Pastor Tim on my cell phone back in Michigan. I told him to get everyone praying at church because my wife was having a hard time and we were under attack by the enemy. Lorie had wanted to go back to Michigan, but I told her we were not going back. We had another day to prepare for Lorie's interview and I prayed constantly.

That morning we prepared to visit Twin Rivers Worship Center in Fenton. We had been invited there by a dear lady who had initially interviewed me at Joyce Meyer Ministries, Andrea deCento. After we arrived and parked the car we found Andrea at the church offices. She introduced us to several staff at the church, including the pastor, and we had a wonderful time of praise and worship, fellowship, and teaching. It was a blessed day for us there. There is nothing like the presence of God to make you feel at home with other believers when you are giving Him praise, no matter what city you are in. We were in the presence of other believers who loved the Lord and it was wonderful. Afterward we went out to eat with Andrea and her daughter Valerie, who had recently moved from the east coast. Lorie and Valerie quickly bonded, and after dinner they were talking up a storm. I knew that God was using Lorie that day to minister to Valerie.

Monday morning we prepared for Lorie's interview at 10:00 am. As we drove to the ministry headquarters we held hands and prayed that God would bless the interview. Within minutes we arrived at the front gate, and after talking to the security guard we were directed to the visitor parking area. I walked in with Lorie and waited a few minutes until she went in to begin the interview. Over an hour later she came out and the human resource manager Carol Pile was with her. It gave us a chance to talk for a few minutes. I told Carol I was looking forward to starting my new job with the ministry after Labor Day. After saying goodbye Lorie and I left and stopped at a nearby apartment complex where we signed a lease and placed a deposit. I had Lorie write and sign the check as a sign of faith that we believed God for our future.

By the time we left Fenton to return to Michigan I knew that Lorie was ready to make whatever sacrifice was required for God's plan to unfold. We were in agreement.

I had been praying that God would soften Lorie's heart and give her peace about the move and all the things she had been dealing with emotionally. By the time we returned to Michigan after our trip God had spoken to her and she was now committed to trust Him. I had read to Lorie Genesis chapter 12 about Abraham, and I continued to remind her of what God had spoken to him, and how He was also speaking to us.

Within a week after our return we went to my parent's home for dinner. We had not told my mother and my step-father the news yet about moving to Missouri. We mentioned to them that we had something to tell them, but we gave them no clue about what was going on. I was filled with anticipation, excitement, and great joy to share this with my mother. She had prayed for me all those years when I did not know God. I knew she would be sad about us leaving, but at the same time she would be filled with joy to know I was going to be a part of a ministry that touches lives all over the world.

That day as we sat with my parents at the dinner table my mother asked me to pray. I laugh now when I say that my mother set a trap for me because when I gave the blessing I thanked the Lord for the plans He had for us. My mother looked at me immediately and said, *"You're going to the mission field aren't you?"* I said yes, and she asked where. When I told her she cried, but they were tears of joy. I could never thank God enough for my mother and the prayers she prayed for me all those years. Even when I was not listening and unreachable she continued to pray and trust God. When I was able to share with her the news about going to Joyce Meyer Ministries I wanted her to know that it was because of her prayers that God finally got my attention one day, and now I was living my life to serve Him and follow the plan He had for my life.

Lorie and I were committed to go to Joyce Meyer Ministries because we knew it has been a ministry that touches people's lives all over the world. God had used Joyce and touched our lives so many times with her books and tapes. It was her book *Approval Addiction* that began the healing in my life leading into Cleansing Stream. Now we were humbled and in awe of everything God had done. I had come to a place in my life where I was ready to sacrifice everything for Him. I had learned how to hear the voice of God speaking to me by living a life of obedience and seeking God with all my heart. Because of that He had given me great favor, and now we were prepared to continue on the path God had set before us.

After everything that happened in our lives over the past months there were several things I needed to take care of. One of my concerns was figuring out how I was going to tell my father that I was leaving him. Suddenly God had brought this tremendous healing in my life and a relationship with my father that I never had before. Now that I was able to see my father each week and minister to him I was going to leave. Not only was my father frail and weak, but he had become attached to me in a way that I never experienced. He had become dependent on me as a sheep is to its shepherd. Each week when I went to visit him and pray over him he began to tell me that he didn't know what he would do without me. In the back of my mind I was trying to determine how I was going to tell him the news. I began to pray that God would bring someone who could go to see my father for me each week to fill the void that would be there after I left.

I also had to write a letter of notice to my present employer and explain the reasons for my sudden departure after having worked for them about three months. By the second week of August I drafted a letter and informed them that by the end of the month I was resigning my position to take a job with Joyce Meyer Ministries (JMM). I went into detail regarding how I applied for a job a year earlier with JMM and interviewed in February. I also explained how I had not heard from the ministry for several months so I took the job I presently had with the intention to stay for a very long time. I explained that after careful consideration with my wife we both felt that this was the right decision. I expressed a fondness for the company and gratitude for their confidence in me while I was there.

Just a few days before I planned to turn in my letter of resignation I wanted to talk to my manager Jerry. He had placed a great deal of trust in me and I was hoping for the opportunity to speak to him personally before meeting with the company Human Resources Manager. It was my intention to talk to Jerry and explain in detail the circumstances for me leaving. For two days he had not been in the office and I felt that it was too important to call him at home to talk to him over the phone. By the following Monday morning I expected him to return to the office as normal so I could meet with him.

I was surprised when Monday came and Jerry was not in the office again. I checked his office several times that morning and had checked to see if anyone knew when he would be coming in. By noon I felt an urgency that I needed to go to the human resources manager to talk to her.

Kim was in her office sitting behind the desk when I stopped by the door and asked if I could have a few minutes of her time. Always friendly and smiling Kim said, *"Sure, come on in."* As I came in I closed the door behind me and suddenly the look on her face became concerned. I sat down holding the letter of resignation in my hand and told her *"I have something I need to give to you."* That lady had the gift of discernment because the next thing she said was, *"It's not your resignation is it?"* As I said yes her mouth fell open, and raising a hand slightly I told her, *"Please read the letter."* She quickly read the letter I handed her and I could see that she did not fully understand. So I went into great detail about applying for the job in Missouri almost a year earlier with the ministry, and I also shared the events that occurred in February and then during the summer. I did not want to give the impression that I had taken a job just for the sake of having something until JMM had called, especially since I received the call when I least expected it.

At that point I expected either one of two things to occur. I thought that she would terminate me on the spot as some companies do when they learn an employee is leaving, or that she would ask me to stay and help with the transition until leaving for Missouri.

What happened next caught me totally by surprise. Kim laid the letter on her desk, and looking straight at me she said, *"What would it take to keep you here."* The statement caught me by surprise. Then the next thing she said just about knocked me off my seat because I had only heard the expression in movies. She said, *"Name your price."* In my mind I thought there is no price because I was going to work for God. Then I explained to Kim that this was a calling in my life from God and that this was something I needed to do. Then I told her I would consider what she had said to me and come back to her office to talk to her later.

At that time Lorie and I had been waiting for a call from Joyce Meyer Ministries regarding the job that Lorie had interviewed for. Our hope and our prayer was that we would both have jobs with the ministry when moving to Missouri and we would become a part of it together. Lorie had called the ministry that morning to check the status of her interview and we were still waiting to hear something back.

I walked back to my office a bit dazed and confused. I was thinking of calling Pastor Keith, and in that moment my phone rang. It was him. He was calling to see if I had submitted my resignation yet. I was thankful for his call because I needed some wisdom at that time to sort out what was going on. I had already determined in my heart that we were leaving for Missouri. Our home was up for sale and we had already begun selling several possessions in preparation for the move.

I explained to Pastor Keith what had happened. Being protective of me he mentioned his concern for me because of my past. He knew that when my past came up with previous employers they would let me go and I would lose my job. I knew his concern was legitimate. If I was supposed to stay then my past should never become an issue. After Pastor Keith prayed with me over the phone I knew that I needed to go back to see Kim and tell her all my concerns, including my past.

About an hour or so had passed since my conversation with Keith. In the meantime I had done some research and gathered some information. Then I went back to the human resource manager's office to talk to her. I still had the full intention of leaving for Missouri to work in the ministry.

After I sat down I pushed some papers across the desk to Kim and I told her that the figures on the paper was the salary I should be making. I also mentioned that at the time my wife Lorie had to wait a year for medical insurance, and if I was going to stay they would have to do something about it. Then I told her, *"Believe it or not, this is not about money."* I began to tell her the story of my past and shared the testimony of my life. I told all about my life as a state trooper falling from grace that led to a life of crime and prison. I explained how Jesus Christ changed my life and the person I had become.

When I finished talking I half expected for her to point and say, *"There's the door."* In the past it seemed like just about every time I had been truthful about my past with employers they would let me go and I lost my job. But what happened next surprised me even more. Kim looked straight at me, and for the first time in my life I heard the words, *"John, your past is not an issue here and it will not become an issue. I believe that you are a man of integrity."* She went on to tell me that I had brought something into the company that was missing, and how I was such a positive person. After heaping praises on me she told me that by noon the next day she was going to have an answer for me, some kind of offer from the company to stay.

When I walked out of the office I was even more confused, and I prayed all the way back to my office, *God what is going on? I don't understand.* After I got to my office I called Lorie at home to tell her what was going on. She was happy about the response from my job, and at the same time she was still struggling about leaving.

After I got off work that day I prayed all the way home, asking God what was I supposed to do. I was very confused with all the recent events and did not understand. I was determined in my heart that we were supposed to go to Missouri, and yet my wife was struggling. Now that I had shared my past with my employer and got a response that I never had before I was even more confused. Within 24 hours I was going to receive an answer from the Lord that I never expected as well.

At 4:30 am the next morning I got up to read my Bible and pray. That morning as I prayed all I could say was *Lord I'm listening.* I opened my journal and wrote those words down. Nothing else came into my mind. I wanted God's will for my life more than anything, more than a place to live, or any job.

After I showered and dressed for work I left the house about 5:15 am to go to a breakfast and meet with some of the men from our church before going to work. At that time in the morning as I drove down the quiet country road we lived on there was no other traffic and I began to hear the voice of God speaking to my heart regarding Abraham. I remembered that as Lorie and I had been preparing to make the long journey to Missouri in recent weeks I reminded her of how God spoke to Abraham and told him to leave his family and possessions, and to go to a country that God had prepared for him. Lorie had been reading that scripture every morning in preparation for our departure.

As God began to speak to my heart He showed me Abraham taking his son Isaac up on a mountain to sacrifice his son's life as an offering to God *(Genesis Chapter 22)*. God had already blessed Abraham with so much after having established his covenant with him, and now he was testing Abraham to see if he would be willing to sacrifice his only son Isaac whom he loved so much. So God commanded Abraham to take the life of Isaac.

In that moment I could see Abraham laying his son Isaac on the alter and raising the knife to take his life out of obedience, and then God stepped in to stop him. Abraham had not withheld what he loved most from the Lord. As God showed me this I heard Him speak the words to my heart, *"You have passed the test."* I then realized that the events of the past 24 hours, when I had gone to my employer to tell them everything about my past was a test for me. God was testing me to see if I was willing to sacrifice everything for Him and be obedient. As the tears ran down my face I was so thankful for this moment in my life when I heard from God and realized that I was living according to the plan He had for my life. This was a precious moment in time that stood still for me to hear the voice of God and receive His favor.

I was the second person to arrive at the men's breakfast after Pastor Keith arrived and I shared with him the events that had taken place and how God had spoken to my heart. He prayed with me and after breakfast I went to work feeling at peace, ready to accept what God had waiting for me.

About an hour before lunch Lorie called me from home. Joyce Meyer Ministries had called her and said that at that time they didn't feel they had a position for her at the ministry. After God spoke to my heart earlier that morning I thought it was confirmation for what was to come.

Thirty minutes later I went to the human resource office and sat down. As I sat across the desk Kim explained to me that she had met with the chief financial officer (CFO) of the company after talking to me a day earlier. Kim explained to her what had taken place and she also contacted my manager Jerry. Then she pushed some papers across the desk with a salary figure. She offered Lorie and me full medical benefits immediately. By the time she finished with their offer for me to stay it amounted to a financial blessing that could only come from God. I learned from Kim that she and the CFO met with the chief executive officer of the company the day before and he gave his approval for the offer they wanted to submit to me. After the events that had taken place I knew I was supposed to stay with the company and I accepted their offer.

I called my wife Lorie after I returned to my office to share the news of what God had done and we both wept tears of gratitude. We were both so thankful that the Lord brought me to a place where I was embraced and accepted regardless of my past. As Lorie and I talked about everything later we realized that God had been speaking to her heart as well and that the Lord had planned for us to stay.

Within a few days I contacted Carol Piles at Joyce Meyer Ministries and explained everything that had happened. She said she understood, and that they were going to keep my application on file. Carol told me that many people have come and interviewed for jobs with the ministry, only to start two or three years later. She told me about one lady who came six years later.

God has placed a seed in my heart to become a part of Joyce Meyer Ministries some day in the future. I don't know when, but God knows. I wrote Joyce a long letter to let her know how her ministry has touched our lives, and how much we love Joyce and her husband Dave.

Until six years before this I had never heard of Joyce Meyer. I never expected that after Lorie introduced me to Joyce's teachings how God would use her ministry to begin healing internal scars and wounds I had been carrying with me all of my life. I've never been the same since.

In the days following my decision to stay in Michigan I wrote in my journal:

I become less, that He (Christ) may become greater in me day by day. I desire to live each day sacrificially for my Lord and my God. "The Angel of the Lord called to Abraham a second time and said, I swear by myself that because you have done this and have not withheld your only son, I will surely bless you and make your descendants as numerous as the stars in the sky and as the sand on the seashore. Your descendants will take possession of the cities of their enemies, and through your offspring all nations on earth will be blessed, because you have obeyed me." Genesis 22:15-19

I believe in my heart that the primary reason God intended for me to stay was my father. He never knew Jesus and now the Lord has been using me to teach my father about the life of Christ and His love for us. I never expected that God would use me to disciple my own father, but that is what He did. Each day that we spent together I took the opportunity to read the Bible with him. I went into great detail to explain what God teaches us through His Word and my father always received it with gladness. I read to him about many different people God used throughout the Bible, men like King David, John the Baptist, and the Apostle Paul. I also prepared my father for the day that he would meet Jesus face to face. My dad received peace that he never had his entire life and each day we spent together I saw a light shining from within his eyes. It was the light of our Lord Jesus. I knew that my father was ready for that day when he would be ushered into the presence of Christ.

God was also using me to touch the lives of people here. He brought me into relationships to minister to other men who have suffered great loss and pain. I don't believe in coincidence where people's lives are concerned. I know that God plans divine appointments for His purposes and He has been using me to sow seeds into the lives of friends and family who have been wounded and are in need of healing.

God has also been preparing me for something greater that I cannot yet explain. I only know that I have sensed it and others have spoken it into my life. Until that day I will continue to follow the path that God has prepared for me, and when all is said and done I can say as the Apostle Paul that I lived wisely.

"For I am already being poured out like a drink offering, and the time has come for my departure. I have fought the good fight, I have finished the race, I have kept the faith. Now there is in store for me the crown of righteousness, which the Lord, the righteous Judge, will award to me on that day— and not only to me, but also to all who have longed for his appearing."2 Timothy 4: 6-8

Chapter 18

Following the months that Lorie and I stayed in Michigan God blessed me with things I had never experienced with my dad. On Christmas day in 2005 I picked him up at the nursing home and took him to church with me. It was the first time in my life that my dad spent Christmas Day worshipping God with me. His body was weak and frail. He only weighed about 70 or 80 pounds. He could not walk or stand, so I took him to the car in a wheelchair, picked him up, and gently put him in the car. I remember taking him from the car into the township hall where Crossfire Ministries was meeting at the time. I introduced him to many people that day and sat him up near the front as we praised and worshipped the Lord. There was a special program that day as Tammy Trent came and sang to several children. I felt like one of those children as I held on tightly to one of my dad's hands. I remember the tears of joy that filled my eyes and gratitude to God that consumed my heart. It is a Christmas that I will never forget.

A few months later spring arrived, then the Easter holiday. When I arrived at the nursing home two Saturdays later my brother Ben was already there wheeling our father down the hallway in a wheel-chair. My father had a glow about him that day. It was a day none of us would ever forget. In the weeks prior to this day I had been reading to him about baptism and had shared with him the story of John the Baptist baptizing our Lord Jesus in the Jordan River. I had explained to my father the importance of baptism and what it meant, that it is a declaration of faith in Jesus Christ. It is a demonstration on the outside of what God has done inside us, changing us into a new person. It is a confession of faith, of commitment to God.

My father had expressed a desire to get baptized before Easter and I had suggested to Ben's wife Michelle that she check if our father could be baptized at their church, which was just a few miles from the nursing home. She made all the arrangements and on a Saturday afternoon we proceeded with the plans.

The week before I had spoken to a nurse who worked on the wing where my father was and she told me to call Steve Schick, who was the Hospice Chaplain. I called him the following day and learned he had visited my father for the first time a week earlier. In his meeting with my father Steve asked him what was the most important thing in life to him, and my father said the Lord. It moved my heart to hear that my father was expressing his faith in God to others. I also learned that he had been telling people that he was going to be baptized and how excited he was about it.

Now on this Saturday afternoon in late April I traveled with my brother Ben and my father to Alpine Baptist church where the baptism was going to take place. We were the first to arrive. After going inside the church I examined the baptismal tank with my brother. It was situated up a stairway behind the main platform of the sanctuary. My father could not walk in his frail condition and I planned to carry him into the tank for the ceremony.

Within a short time other people began to arrive. My wife Lorie came and brought cameras so we could photograph this special time. My sister and her husband also arrived. Ben's wife Michelle and four of their children came too, and one of my father's few remaining family, his sister Barbara. Chaplain Steve Schick from Hospice arrived with the head Hospice nurse Charlene, and the Hospice social worker.

The pastor arrived and I went over the details of the ceremony with him. I changed clothes and talked to my father to see if he was ready. After pushing his wheelchair to the stairway I picked him up in my arms. He still only weighed about 70 pounds so he wasn't heavy. I climbed the short stairway behind the pastor and we entered the heated tank. Once we stepped down into the water I lowered my father enough so he could stand and hold onto me for support. The pastor from my brother's church had visited our father on other occasions and knew of his faith in Christ. Now here in front of family and other witnesses the pastor asked him about when he gave his life to the Lord and my dad professed his faith in Christ. As I held my father and the pastor pronounced him baptized in the name of Jesus we lowered him together until submersed, and when my father came up out of the water his face was bright and shiny. He exclaimed how good it felt, and as our family and friends looked on shouting and clapping my father spoke and thanked them for coming. It was a moment I could never picture a year before, but God had appointed this time.

After I picked my father up and carried him down the stairs to a changing room my brother Ben helped me dry him off and get him into some dry clothes. A few minutes later Ben stepped out of the room, and the first thing my dad said to me was, *"I felt like I was born again."* I said, *"Yes Dad, you were."* I was so thankful to the Lord for this day and time. Looking at my father I could only see him as the Lord saw him. The man he once was had surely died.

(Brother Ben, John, and Ben Sr. after Baptism)

In the days following the baptism I met more of the nursing staff that worked at the home where my father lived. All of them expressed to me what a profound change they had witnessed in him. One of the nurses, Cindy Lowry, was also a member of my church. Previously I did not even know she worked there until I saw her one day when I was visiting my father. She was as surprised as I was because she knew who my father was, but she did not know that I was his son. I had shared with Cindy about my father getting baptized and she was very excited for him. A few weeks later Cindy had an opportunity to testify in my church about Cleansing Stream. She and her husband had gone through the classes and just finished the weekend retreat. Part of her testimony reflected on the healing that she had seen in many people, and she spoke about my father. She spoke of what a bitter man he had been when he first came to the nursing home and how the Lord had changed him and changed his heart. It made me remember the first time I had seen my father outside my brother Ben's shop almost six years earlier when he did not recognize me at first because Christ was living in me and the person I was on the outside was different than what he had seen in the past. My eyes welled up with tears as I realized that the countenance of my father had also changed. Those who had known him years ago as a bitter and angry man would not recognize him now because of the light and love of Jesus that lived in him.

There was a quiet peace of God that covered my father during the remaining days of his life. Hospice had been caring for him and I recognized changes in his physical body as he deteriorated and weakened. He ate less and less, but he never complained of pain or discomfort. I sensed that he knew the end was near. On the days that I visited him and tried to feed him he would eat only a small bite or two of food. Yet he always remained strong enough to listen as I read to him the Word of God and prayed with him. As we studied together he always thanked me for reading and praying. He understood what God was teaching him and he received it with gladness.

God had used me for over a year to disciple my father. At one time I never would have thought it possible, but I have witnessed that God can do the impossible when it seems that there may be no hope. The angry and hardened heart of a man who once cursed God had become broken and molded into a new heart that was soft for God and caring for others. In *Ezekiel 36:26* it says, *"I will give you a new heart and put a new spirit in you."* That is exactly what the Lord had done with my father. Just over a year earlier when I had been healed of the pain and fear of rejection that I carried all of my life I believed it was the greatest healing that God had performed in my life and it was a miracle. Since that day I came to see my father and confront him about his eternal destiny and we prayed the prayer of salvation I witnessed a greater miracle than my healing. It became even more apparent to me in the weeks before my father died. My father's heart had been completely healed by God. He now had the heart of Jesus. He cared more for every person who came in contact with him and expressed concern for their needs instead of his own.

Less than a week before he died I visited him and immediately recognized he was flushed and weakening quickly. I did not know the day or the time that his physical body would give out, but I could tell it was going to be soon. God had given me strength to always remain calm when I saw my father in his weakened condition. When I asked him if he was alright he never complained. He would never ask for anything, but he would gladly accept a cold Coca Cola from the vending machine. It was his only vice. Each time I came to see him he never asked for it, but when I offered to buy him a Coke he would just say *"If you don't mind, sure."* He didn't want to burden me in any way, but it was my chance to do some small thing for him. It was one of the simple things in life that he enjoyed and it pleased me to provide something for him that he appreciated so much. I would hold the bottle and straw for him as he took a long sip and recognized the satisfied look on his face as the cold drink went down his throat. He was so thankful for such a small thing. Even on past occasions when I had visited him I had heard from nurses and aides who cared for him how grateful he was for small things. One of the nurses named Marianne told me one day how much my father appreciated a piece of toast in the morning with peanut butter on it. She shared with me how my dad had thanked her and told her how much it meant to him. I could see that it touched her heart and she was one of many that cared about him.

The day before Father's Day I went to see my father again and his voice was barely a whisper. There was a car show being held outside the facility for the residents and I wanted to take my father out to see the antique cars. I had promised him just a day before that I would return to take him. When I arrived two of the Hospice aides told me they tried to take him out but he said, *"No, my son will be coming to take me."* So many of the staff there had been touched by my father and they had become fond of him. In the past few months I had met many staff who approached me about my father to tell me what a wonderful man he was, how he was gentle and kind. Not only did they care for him, but they genuinely cared about him. I took great comfort in leaving after each visit to know that he was in a place where he not only gave love but he received it.

That particular day was hot and muggy. Two of the aides came down to my father's room to dress him and put him in a wheel chair for me to take him outside. Both knew him by name and treated him with loving kindness. When I took him outside in the midday sun his head hung down from a lack of strength and the brightness of the sun was beaming upon him. I put my sunglasses on him to give him some shade and wheeled him around each antique car for a close look. My father had always loved old cars and had a passion for them ever since I was a child.

As we went around each car to see the inside and look under the hood he was so weak he could not lift his head so I knelt next to him to lift his head and help him see better. I sensed that in his weakness he was allowing me to show him all the cars because he thought it pleased me. There were some motorcycles there too and after we looked at the cars I wheeled my father around the motorcycles. I remembered how fond he had also been of them when I was a boy. When I was four years old my father owned a Triumph motorcycle. He spoke of it many times in years past and he even mentioned it on this day. I remember him taking me for rides those many years ago, putting me on the gas tank as he sat behind me.

My father could not eat that day. I took him to a tent they had setup outside and tried to feed him, but he only took a small bite and would not take any more. I could tell that he was already exhausted and took him back into the facility to his room. After the aides put him back in his bed I could see that he was tired and I prayed over him. When I finished and we both said Amen I looked my father in the eye to tell him, *"Dad, I want you to know that I am proud to be your son."* He just looked back with a smile and whispered, *"I hope so."* I was also very proud of my father for the man he had become in Christ. God had given to my father that peace that surpasses all understanding. I saw that my father had placed his faith and trust in the living God and that he was ready for the journey that would take him from this life to an eternal resting place with our Lord Jesus.

The following Tuesday evening my brother Ben called me. He had received a call from the nursing home that our father had a fever and had been vomiting. He was having difficulty breathing. As I drove there I prayed and asked the Lord to give my father comfort. Upon arriving I saw my brother Ben standing next to the bed holding my father's hand. Oxygen tubes were attached to him and his breathing was labored. He was very warm with fever and I saw that he was fading in and out of consciousness. I took his other hand to sit next to him and his eyes opened slightly. He recognized me and squeezed my hand. The Hospice nurse scheduled for the next shift had come in early and was checking his temperature again as Ben and I stood watching. I held the thermometer under my father's tongue and moments later the nurse told us his temperature was coming down. He seemed calmer now and was aware that Ben and I were there with him. I could see the concern on my brother's face, but somehow I felt that it was not yet time for our father to leave us. I asked my dad if I could read to him and he nodded yes. Then I opened my Bible and began to read.

"If I speak in the tongues of men and of angels, but have not love, I am only a resounding gong or a clanging cymbal. If I have the gift of prophecy and can fathom all mysteries and all knowledge, and if I have a faith that can move mountains, but have not love, I am nothing. If I give all I possess to the poor and surrender my body to the flames, but have not love, I gain nothing.

Love is patient, love is kind. It does not envy, it does not boast, it is not proud. It is not rude, it is not self-seeking, it is not easily angered, it keeps no record of wrongs. Love does not delight in evil but rejoices with the truth. It always protects, always trusts, always hopes, always perseveres.

Love never fails. But where there are prophecies, they will cease; where there are tongues, they will be stilled; where there is knowledge, it will pass away. For we know in part and we prophesy in part, but when perfection comes, the imperfect disappears. When I was a child, I talked like a child, I thought like a child, I reasoned like a child. When I became a man, I put childish ways behind me. Now we see but a poor reflection as in a mirror; then we shall see face to face. Now I know in part; then I shall know fully, even as I am fully known.

And now these three remain: faith, hope and love. But the greatest of these is love." (I Corinthians 13)

As I read the scriptures I knew that my father was filled with the love of Christ. I had seen it in his beaming face and so had others. I witnessed it in his caring and concern for everyone but himself. The love of Jesus gave him total peace and confidence in God.

In *1 John 4* it says, *"If anyone acknowledges that Jesus is the Son of God, God lives in him and he in God. And so we know and rely on the love God has for us…There is no fear in love. But perfect love drives out fear…"* The love of Christ that sustained my father also gave him courage to face the inevitable. He knew that the end was near for his physical body, and yet in his weakness God had made him strong. As my brother and I sat on either side of the bed next to our father we held hands and I began to pray. I asked the Lord to give my father strength, comfort, and peace. As I hugged and kissed my father before leaving I told him that I loved him and he whispered the same words to me.

On my way home I called my sister Micki and told her of the events of that evening. She was very concerned and went there that night to stand vigil over our father. The following day I went to the nursing home again and my sister was still there. She had spent most of the night with our father and had left in the early morning hours to go home and sleep for awhile. Upon seeing my father his deep blue eyes were fading as he lay in bed with the oxygen tube under his nostrils. He was resting comfortably and he seemed more alert. As I sat down next to him and took his hand in mine I asked him if he wanted a cold Coke and he nodded yes. Before I left the room I had a chance to talk to my sister about the events of the early morning and she handed me some literature from Hospice regarding signs of impending death. She had been crying. I could tell by the look on her face how deeply this was affecting her. A few minutes later I left the room to go get a cold soft drink at the employee break room and on my way I stopped at the office at the end of the wing to speak to the Hospice Social Worker and the nurse Cindy Lowry who was from my church. We talked about my father's condition and they were not sure if he was experiencing symptoms of flu or if it was a sign of impending death. They mentioned the literature I received from my sister and suggested that I study and read regarding signs that my father's life may be ending soon. Whatever God's purpose was at that time I knew my father was prepared. After I went to the employee break room and returned to my father's room I sat at his bedside and gave him a sip of the cold drink. He took a tiny taste, but it was enough to refresh him. I opened my Bible as I had on every visit to read to my father. We had talked many times about eternal life with Jesus and my father knew what was to come. He was not afraid and he believed it in his heart. I read to him once again the scripture I had shared with him many times before from *John 14 (v. 1-6)*,

"Do not let your hearts be troubled. Trust in God; trust also in me. In my Father's house are many rooms; if it were not so, I would have told you. I am going there to prepare a place for you. And if I go and prepare a place for you, I will come back and take you to be with me that you also may be where I am. You know the way to the place where I am going." Thomas said to him, "Lord, we don't know where you are going, so how can we know the way?" Jesus answered, "I am the way and the truth and the life. No one comes to the Father except through me."

My father understood and believed those words. I asked him if he was ready to go to Heaven and he said yes. I also asked him if he could feel the presence of the Holy Spirit and he nodded yes again. I knew that as the time grew near in these final hours of my father's life he was ready to approach the throne of God with confidence.

God also showed me how to teach my father one last thing that day. It is the universal expression of praise to God spoken by millions of people around the world who may not share the same language or culture. It is the simple expression of faith and praise. It is the word h*allelujah*. That day my father spoke the word *hallelujah* for the first time.

One last time I took the opportunity to pray with my father the prayer that Jesus had taught the disciples in *Luke Chapter 11*, the same prayer that I had said with my father for the first time months earlier, *The Lord's Prayer.* After we prayed together I laid my hands on my father's head and prayed over him with my sister. Holding tightly to my hands he whispered *Amen* with me and told me he loved me. I hugged my father and kissed his head and told him again how much I loved him too. When I left the room I praised God, knowing that my father was ready for the journey from this life that would take him to the presence of Christ. Those were the last words I heard from my father.

Later that same night my brother Ben had stayed with our father until 10:30 pm. When Ben left to go home our father was resting peacefully. We learned later that just after midnight he breathed his last breath. He had not been in any pain or suffering. I believe that the time was appointed by God. My father did not want anyone to cry or be in grief over his leaving. Hours before when my sister had been with him she had cried and in his selfless state he said to her, *"Don't cry Sis..."* Our humble father was more concerned for the welfare of another. He had for some time affectionately referred to his daughter as *Sis,* and in his final hours he did not want her to shed tears for him.

Chapter 19

Two days later I attended a prophesy conference with members of the worship team from my church. We were scheduled to lead praise and worship for the conference. The leader of our group had excused me from coming because of my father's passing, but I felt an urgency to attend. I sensed that God was going to speak into my heart or show me something regarding my father. Earlier in the week when I had been in prayer for my father I could hear God speaking to me with the words of comfort, *"I'm here."* I longed to hear or see something from God that would tell me more regarding my father. Before the conference began I was praying with our worship team outside the sanctuary. Our pastor Judy was leading us in prayer before the worship was to begin for the conference. She began to pray that God would provide a path leading up a mountain that led to Him and that people would be drawn to that path. A short time later after praise and worship began I sensed the presence of the Holy Spirit entering the sanctuary and God showed me a vision of my father. I saw the path leading up a mountain and the majesty of God shined brilliantly from the top. As I looked again I saw my father walking up the path. Then he stopped to look back at me. The light of God was upon his face as he looked at me and smiled. There was a great peace and joy that covered him. Then I looked again and saw someone holding his hand. It was Jesus and he was leading my father up the mountain. The Lord smiled upon my father and tears came down my face as I was overwhelmed with thankfulness and joy. I knew that my father had finally reached the place in eternity with Jesus where I will see him again one day.

The following Monday the memorial service for my father was being held at my brother Ben's church. To honor our father's wishes there was no funeral and his remains were cremated. I had been preparing over the weekend in prayer and meditating on God's Word. I had received words of encouragement and hugs from several people from our church on Sunday. Now I looked forward to sharing with people the story of what God had done in my father's life.

The pastor from my brother's church was away on vacation at the time so my sister Micki, my brother Ben and I agreed to ask the hospice chaplain to lead the memorial service. Chaplain Steve had developed a close relationship with our father while he was in the nursing home and he had been present when our father was baptized. He had personally seen the man our father had become and knew his heart for God. He was there at the nursing home the morning we discovered that our father had died. He prayed with us and gave us comfort. It pleased us greatly when we asked him to conduct the memorial service and he gladly accepted.

That Monday morning I arrived at the church with my wife Lorie just after 10:00 am. The service was due to start in an hour and my sister was already there in the sanctuary preparing some of the flower arrangements. As the time drew near to 11:00 and people arrived and came in I was happy to see so many people that my father had known through friendships, his work, and from the nursing home.

It touched my heart to meet Cindy Lowry's 16 year-old daughter Jessica. She had known my father and had visited him many times, and according to Cindy her daughter had become very fond of my father. The love of Jesus that had filled my father touched her in a very special way. As I shook Jessica's hand and thanked her for coming I could see the well of tears that filled her eyes with sadness because of the grief she felt from my father's passing.

Chaplain Steve began the service and spoke of the gentle and kind man he had come to know and see in my father. He shared the miracle of Christ living in my father and spoke the words that I had shared with my father after he gave his life to Christ, that *"If any man be in Christ he is a new creation. The past is gone. Behold everything has become new."* *(2 Corinthians 5:17)* There had been times when my father expressed how sorry he was for past wrongs, but when I read the scripture to him I explained that since God had made him a new creation that person he once was never existed. God had washed away his sins and gave him a new life. My father was indeed a new man. The new life he had in Christ was not based on his past.

My sister's grief had been the shedding of many tears and the telling of stories that I had long ago forgotten. I knew that she had carried her own pain from the past as I had before God completely healed me the year before, but I never understood completely until that day. My sister had always yearned for the love of her father. She was *daddy's little girl.* She told of our father's love for animals, cars, and motorcycles ever since we could remember as children, and how precious they were to him. He was gifted at training horses to do tricks and when we were kids he had a dog that he loved. He enjoyed going to horse auctions. He would buy wild horses to break and train, then sell them. I could faintly remember those times, and as my sister talked about them the memories began to flood back into my mind. As a small girl of about seven years old she begged our father to take her with him to a horse auction. When he agreed and she went with him that day she spotted a small donkey barely old enough to leave it's mother. Micki told of how she begged our father to buy that donkey for her and how he finally gave in. She promised to feed and care for it and our father finally agreed. He didn't bring a trailer that day so he took the back seat out of the car and put the baby donkey in. His cars were always immaculate, and this was an older car that he loved dearly. It was impeccable in appearance inside and out because of the care our father gave it. All the way home that baby donkey cried and kicked against the back doors and the interior. It was quite a mess. But our father showed love to his little girl that day. A week later my sister recalled that the baby donkey had died and that our father told her it was just too young to leave its mother. Tearfully she shared that it was the first time that our father cried with her. Not long after that our parents divorced and she was separated from our dad. For years her relationship with him was never what she hoped for as our father had become a bitter and angry man. Their relationship became strained and my sister carried that pain most of her life. Tears covered my eyes as I listened to my sister speak of the years she had missed having a father's love and never being able to get close to him. She talked briefly about the man he once had been and how angry he was after having to go into a nursing home. Over two years earlier our father had been forgetting things. In the early stages of his dementia he would turn a stove on to boil water and forget about it, or pay a bill and forget he paid it then pay it again. Then when my sister and brother Ben recognized that something was definitely wrong they took our father to the hospital where they found out he had a stroke. After being hospitalized he had two more strokes and his condition deteriorated. Family had tried to care for him after he was released from the hospital but it became impossible to give him the care he needed. When there was no choice but to put him in a nursing home he became very angry and mean. It was during that time that he cursed my younger brother Randy who had the unbearable task of taking him to one of the nursing homes. Our father had become so unmanageable that he went from one nursing home to another before he finally ended up staying at St. Mary's Rehabilitation Center. Even after he arrived there his anger and rebellious spirit got him in trouble. My sister told how she had received a call from the nursing home because our father tried to pick a fight with another older man in the cafeteria. It was like a call from the principal of the school calling a parent because of a troubled child. Our father had been banned from the cafeteria for some time for that incident. For a long time he resented everyone and everything around him. But my sister acknowledged that a change began to take place in our father sometime after that, when I went to see him at St. Mary's nursing home to confront him about his life and tell him why God had sent me to see him. Since that day when I prayed the sinner's prayer with my father and he wept with me in my arms God began to do more than any of us could have ever imagined. Until my sister spoke that day at the memorial service I didn't realize that the Lord also began to bring healing to my sister. God had restored the relationship my sister Micki had longed for with our father. She had become *daddy's little girl* again. Less than two days before his passing when I called her on the phone that previous Tuesday night after 10:00 and she went to the nursing home she told of how she climbed in bed next to dad to cover him and just hold on to him.

When my sister had finished speaking at the memorial service I was awed at what God had done in her life with our father as well. The Lord had brought restoration to a relationship that had for years been strained and almost broken. The pain and loss that my sister felt turned to healing and great gain. God had given her peace as well. There was closure.

I was honored to speak about my father and proclaim that I was his first child and his oldest son. I spoke only briefly about the man my father once was and focused on the last 14 months of his life. Some of the people that attended the service were former co-workers and friends my father associated with in his drinking days. The man they had known ceased to exist when my father surrendered his life to Christ. I doubt that they would have recognized him as the same man had they taken the opportunity to visit him in his last days.

God had given me a relationship with my father that I had longed for since the day I gave my life to Christ. It was a bond established by the Lord the day my father gave his heart to Jesus. I considered everything that we were able to do together for the first time in the last months of my father's life as more precious that any other. Each time God opened my father's heart to receive the Lord was also giving something to me. There were many first-time moments I will forever be thankful for, such as our first prayer together (salvation), the first time we spoke the *Lord's Prayer (Matthew 6: 9-14)*, our first Christmas in church, my father's baptism, the first time I sang to my father, and the first time my father said *halleluiah* less than 24 hours before his passing.

I talked about all of these things at the memorial service and afterwards I realized that God actually brought healing to some hearts in the sanctuary that day. One of my mother's sisters approached me afterwards with tears in her eyes. She is a godly woman who loves the Lord. She confessed to me that for years she had bitterness in her heart toward my father. But on this day she heard how God had changed my father and transformed him. She told me that she had to ask the Lord to forgive her and she asked my forgiveness as well.

I hugged her and realized that God gave her healing and freedom from bitterness.

A year before my father went to be with the Lord I was preparing to leave Michigan and join Joyce Meyer Ministries in Fenton, Missouri. After passing the tests that God had placed before me I realized that I was supposed to stay here to do His will. Since then the Lord gave me precious time with my father that I will never forget as long as I live. When I see my dad again on the day that I join him with our Heavenly Father it will probably seem to him like only a moment ago, for God's Word says, *"But do not forget this one thing, dear friends: With the Lord a day is like a thousand years, and a thousand years are like a day." (2 Peter 3:8)*

In the weeks and months after the memorial service I witnessed the power of God working through my sister Micki. The Lord had used our father's life as a testimony to her personally and spoke to her heart. God was tugging on her, and through the powerful healing that she received Micki gave her heart completely to the Lord. Five months after our father's remains were laid to rest I sat with the rest of our family at Resurrection Life Church in Grandville, Michigan watching my sister and her husband Tony being baptized. In that moment when I saw my sister come up out of the water with her hands raised up to God I thought of our father and I remembered that same light I saw shining upon him.

Chapter 20

I am no longer driven to achieve the things that I once considered personal achievement. I am now called by God to follow the path he has set before me. No longer do I have to carry the pain and sorrow of my past. No one should live with the fear of rejection that I lived with most of my life. Yet there are so many that carry the same scars today that are left from a father or mother that never gave their approval to a son or a daughter. There is emptiness and a longing for acceptance. As you read this book God may be speaking the same words to you that He spoke to me, *"I have chosen you, and not rejected you."* God wants each of us to trust Him with all our hearts, and to accept Him as our Father. Only Jesus Christ can fill that emptiness and tear down the walls many of us have built up around ourselves.

As we walk through life looking for purpose there is a key to finding out what the future is. God knows and He will show you as you call upon Him. He says, *"You will seek me and find me when you seek me with all your heart." (Jeremiah 29:13)* Jesus is the living water, given freely for each of us so that we will never thirst and chase after things in life that cannot fill us with purpose and fulfill-ment. Our destiny is revealed when we receive Him as our Lord and Savior.

When I look back at my life and see a man sitting in a prison cell as a reflection of his father I am in awe of the God who spared my life. When I lived in a place where I was hated and despised I never knew if I would live one minute to the next. I had witnessed others who were beaten, stabbed, and I had seen death. How could it be that the Lord of all Creation spared me and spoke to me in such a way to change me? Before I was born He designed my life, my being, and my purpose. I live because of Him, and I am forever thankful for every breath I take in His presence.

For every person that God used as a seed in my life I will always be thankful. I know that the Lord listened to the prayers of my mother all the years that I was living my life in rebellion. There is nothing more precious than those of a loving mother praying for a son or daughter. Thank you Mom. You were the one who taught me to *"Trust in the Lord with all your heart, and lean not on your own understanding. Acknowledge Him and in your ways and He will direct your paths."(Proverbs 3:5, 6)*

The brightest light that ever shined in a prison was Richard Amo. I am especially thankful to God that He used Richard to be a spiritual father to me at a time in my life when I was very fragile as a young Christian searching for many answers. God used Richard to show that nothing is impossible with Christ. Sentenced to live the rest of his life in prison Richard was given his freedom and spent his life serving the Lord. God had special plans for Richard and had been using him to reach out to inmates in Florida prisons with the love of Jesus. I have been proud to call him my friend. During the time that I wrote this book I learned that he passed away and is now with the Lord. There is a very special place in my heart for him, and I will never forget the days we walked together in a prison yard, and that wonderful day I saw him when he came to celebrate my marriage with Lorie.

Unless a person knew God they would never understand how or why a police officer would come into a prison to minister to inmates. Charlie Myers will always be a big man with a bigger heart. For all the years he came into Muskegon Correctional Facility he reached out with the love of Jesus to touch the lost and he touched my life. I could never imagine years ago that God would bring me together with Charlie as a free man. I am especially thankful that the Lord brought us together in men's ministry and used our experience as a testimony to other men.

It's difficult to imagine a beautiful woman coming into a prison to minister and sing to men behind bars, but that is what Judy Buffum-Hemmila did when she came into Muskegon Correctional Facility with Charlie Myers years ago. She planted a seed in my life that also touched me with the love of Jesus. Today Judy is co-pastor of our church at Crossfire Ministries with her husband Keith. She is also a chaplain for Women of Faith, which is a faith-based women's organization encouraging woman of all ages and stages in life to grow in faith and spiritual maturity through a relationship with Jesus Christ and an understanding of God's love and grace. The ministry holds Revolve conferences for young women and teens all over the United States.

God used countless others to sew seeds into my life as well through volunteers, books, tape ministries, and churches like Resurrection Life Church in Grandville, Michigan. It was there that the common-sense teaching of Pastor Duane VanderKlok helped me grow in my understanding of God's Word and taught me how to apply it to my own life.

It was also at Resurrection Life Church that I met my beautiful wife Lorie. At a time in my life when I least expected it God brought her into my life and changed the desires of my heart. I knew she was the right one for me because God chose her. I am blessed beyond measure for the life that God has given us.

For all the seeds that Joyce Meyer planted in my life I will always be thankful. Since being introduced to her teaching over six years ago God has used Joyce to touch my life beyond measure. It was through her books, tapes, and teachings that the most important healing of my life began with my father.

If my wife Lorie and I had never gone to Crossfire Ministries where Pastor Keith and his wife Judy are pastors we would not have been introduced to Cleansing Stream Ministries. It was here that Cleansing Stream changed my life forever. Mere words cannot express how thankful I am that God used this ministry to heal the scars of my past and give me a relationship with my father that I never dreamed possible. I no longer live for the approval of any man because my heavenly Father will never reject me.

Years ago as a young boy growing up I lived with imaginary heroes. I always hoped that my hero would be a real person one day.

Not only would my hero save others but he would save me too. I can say now that I have a real life hero named Jesus Christ. He saved my life and He lives in me today.

God knew when to bring the right person into my life at the right time, and I will forever be thankful for Chaplain Robert A. Hall and his wife Jamie from Forgotten Man Ministries. It was in the Grand Traverse County jail in December 1991 where God used Chaplain Bob to touch my life and lead me to the Lord. Bob and his wife Jamie have touched hundreds, if not thousands, of men and women in jails and prisons, and in the communities they served. For over 50 years Chaplain Bob Hall dedicated his life to the ministry of sharing Jesus Christ to men and women. In April of 2000 Bob performed the marriage ceremony for my wife Lorie and me. It was always our joy and privilege to visit him and Jamie at their home on the farm in Traverse City, Michigan for fellowship, a good meal, and just enjoying the time together. On many occasions I have been honored to go into the jail where I was an inmate those many years ago to tell my story to the men and women, and to let them know of the love of Christ, and the hope only Jesus gives. Such was the case on July 3, 2007 when Lorie and I went to Traverse City and met Chaplain Bob at the jail. It was the first time his wife Jamie was not with us, as she was in the hospital recovering from surgery. We had a wonderful time together with the men and women, and afterwards, as always, we shared hugs with Bob, expressed our love, and went on our way. We stopped at the hospital to see Jamie shortly after, then left that night. Just a few days later, as Lorie and I were returning home from a trip to northern Michigan I received a call from Jamie telling me that Bob had suffered a massive brain aneurysm and passed away.

The following week Lorie and I returned to Traverse City for the funeral of my beloved friend and mentor. As we entered the main entrance of the church a crowd of people surrounded a memorial, and a police honor guard stood at Chaplain Bob's casket. We greeted family and made our way to the line of people near his wife Jamie, and I looked at several photos of his life and remembered the wonderful times he spent with me. One thing I realized that I was going to miss the most about him was the hugs he always gave me when he greeted me and when we parted. It was time for our final farewell until that day we meet again with the Lord. I heard many wonderful stories that day, listened to some of Bob's favorite hymns, and listened to the testimonies of many people whose lives were changed by knowing the man Robert A. Hall. As one man wrote,

> *"...By far you are the greatest man I have ever known, and you will only realize the impact that your life has had upon mine when all is laid before us in eternity and 'we will know even as we are known.'*
>
> *You are my spiritual mentor, father, and friend. I love you with a love that does not cause me to grieve as 'those who have no hope'...my love causes me to long even more for that wonderful day when I shed this tent (my physical body) and join you in the presence of the Lord.*
>
> *Your conversations will be deeply missed, but I rejoice in my spirit for you. You lived your life longing for the moment when you could stand before the Lord, and just as the Apostle Paul was able to say, 'For I am now ready to be offered, and the time of my departure is at hand. I have fought a good fight, I have finished my course, I have kept the faith'...*

Lorie and I were honored to be asked to be with the family in prayer before the service and to attend the burial with them as well afterward. I was awed to see the 30-40 police officers that came to honor Bob, and when the funeral ended all of the officers formed two lines outside the foyer, standing at attention to salute as the casket passed by. They honored Bob as one of their own. When we left the church in the procession later on my eyes filled with tears of gratitude for how God had used this simple man to touch my life so deeply. The police escort through the city was very evident, as traffic was blocked at every intersection by police cars.

(Chaplain Bob, Jamie, Lorie, and John at the farm)

With every ending there is a new beginning. Some are painful and some are joyful. Since the day I gave my heart to my Lord Jesus in a jail cell over 15 years ago I have witnessed many new beginnings because of the power and love of God at work in others. I have experienced and seen healings that can only be described as miracles. Many times God has spoken things into my life through others and He has always confirmed it. Such was the case with this book. I pray that for every person who reads this God will show you that He is a God who restores and only Jesus can heal the brokenhearted and remove the scars that remain from a father or mother who never gave their approval to a son or daughter. For God is the true Father of all.

References

[1] H.L. Roush, Sr., *Jesus Loves Me,* Reprint of ed. Published by Roush, Belpre, Ohio, 1978, p. 105

Booking Information:

We would like to hear from you. Please write to us or contact us by e-mail if you would like to have John Collier come to your church, ministry, or organization to speak and share his story of the incredible journey that God has taken him on. We want to encourage you to know that *"...nothing is impossible with God." (Luke 1:37)*

Fathers Love Ministries
P.O. Box 264
Rockford, Michigan 49341
e-mail: info@flministry.net

Visit us on the web at <u>flministry.net</u>

Printed in the United States
121410LV00004B/1-132/P

9 781604 773408